RAPID WEIGHT
HYPNOSIS FOR WOMEN

Extreme Weight Loss, Burning Fat Fast and
Naturally. Stop Craving Sugar and Emotional Eating
with Powerful Self-Hypnosis Meditation and
Positive Affirmations

By

DARLENE MCDANIEL

Disclaimer Notice:

Please note the information contained within this document is for educational and entertainment purposes only. All effort has been executed to present accurate, up to date, and reliable, complete information. No warranties of any kind are declared or implied. Readers acknowledge that the author is not engaging in the rendering of legal, financial, medical, or professional advice. The content within this book has been derived from various sources. Please consult a licensed professional before attempting any techniques outlined in this book.

By reading this document, the reader agrees that under no circumstances is the author responsible for any losses, direct or indirect, which are incurred as a result of the use of the information contained within this document, including, but not limited to, — errors, omissions, or inaccuracies.

Table of Contents

CHAPTER FIVE

DAILY WEIGHT LOSS MOTIVATION WITH MINI HABITS

CONCLUSION

INTRODUCTION

Everyone needs to know how much more weight they should lose. Crash diets are just a cause of dissatisfaction when more money is lost and more weight is put back on. So why are so many people dealing with this weight problem, and why are so many people putting more and more weight on it as the years go by?

Well, this could be a very long and in-depth book, but we're not going to get into all the "nitty-gritty" as to why this happens; there are so many explanations, and we could actually be here for days looking into all the whys and how this issue is. The thing that I think needs to be noted is that there are different causes for being overweight and, in some cases, obese. 66.3% of all people are overweight or obese, according to the National Center for Health Statistics in the United States. It's a stunning figure.

Let's take a quick view of some of the reasons why people are struggling with weight loss. It's a relentless fight for so many people, and they feel they've already lost on the word "go." Your quality of life is impaired when you're overweight, and you just don't feel good about yourself. In fact, you feel downright rotten, useless, and just not worth anyone's time of day, so we see how the destructive cycle goes on. You eat for comfort and just keep gaining more weight, leaving you feeling bad about yourself after each and every bite. You know you don't even need to, but you just can't help yourself.

Stress is also thought to cause weight gain. Now, before we all sit back and think that another lesson on comfort food is on its way, let's look at why weight gain happens when you're under stress. Well, cortisol affects one's own weight as well as weight loss. Cortisol is a hormone that is discharged in one's body when it's under stress — which is why it has been called the "stress hormone" — because of the "fight or flight " response that is released in all of us. As far as it concerns weight, that's why the body holds on to weight the way it does.

Some drugs cause weight gains, such as birth control pills, hormones, and antidepressants. The right way to act is to contact your health care professional and let him / her change your prescription to suit your body's needs and prevent you from continuing to gain extra weight. Unfortunately, lifestyle is the greatest cause of weight gain and is why people struggle so hard to shed unnecessary weight. Regrettably, there is no "miracle pill" or "miracle patch" that will just lose those pounds. We live in a time of convenience, with "take-aways" and "drive-thrus" becoming our normal place to have a meal. This is the standard instead of the exception to the rule. They're enticing us at almost every street corner, they're filling us faster than any health snack, and, let's face it, even though the nutritional value on a scale of one to ten is maybe one, we don't really think about it because it tastes good enough and it's easily available. Exercise seems to be too much work, and we don't always have time for it either. Diets are just a pain in the ass, and who knows what we're actually doing to our bodies in the long run with all those medicines that go with it? Just as food is used to cope with depression, grief, stress, and anxiety, it is also used to celebrate and enjoy life. What goes hand in hand when celebrating with food is alcohol, and it is well known that high alcohol intake is often responsible for weighting around the belly.

At the end of the day, we're going back to the value of getting a positive body image. Overweight seems to be arbitrary, and we all place on ourselves (thanks, of course, to the media and society) these very unreasonable standards of what we should look like. However, we should take more care of how much we should weigh for no other reason than health concerns associated with being overweight. High cholesterol, diabetes, heart disease, respiratory issues, and so on are all items to watch out for that have a detrimental impact on your health when you are overweight.

Sensitivity to different foods can also cause fluid retention and weight gain; tests can be performed to see whether there are foods that do not respond well to your system. Symptoms that will arise immediately after eating if you are allergic to this particular food include headaches, indigestion, joint pain, nausea, constipation, diarrhea, and respiratory problems. As problematic as it might be to try not to compromise your eating habits, skip the "drive-thru". When you feel overwhelmed, as tempting as it might be to hit food, go for a walk or jog to get rid of those feelings of rage and frustration. A punching bag is an excellent source of stress relief, so maybe look into investing in one of them and go and pound it instead. The exercise is awesome. I know it's hard to get into the workout, but don't place any unreasonable expectations on yourself when you do it again. The lack of instant results is what holds us off so much. Drink plenty of water, put away the enticing food, and get into a well-balanced eating plan explicitly planned for you by a dietician or health practitioner. Remember that you want to be safe for yourself and your family, and that's how you can make the best move forward from the start.

In this book, you will get to understand how your mindset can change your body positively and how you can change your mindset through self-hypnosis. Also, you will learn the techniques for achieving great weight loss by mindfully eating, as well as through positive affirmations and motivations. The techniques and benefits will help and guide you to achieve your desired and enviable body if followed properly. We are starting with the mindset to change your body and the secret to weight loss in the next chapter.

CHAPTER ONE

HOW YOUR MINDSET CHANGES YOUR BODY – THE SECRET FOR WEIGHT LOSS

There's a lot to say for healthy food and physical exercise, but that alone isn't going to take your health to a newlevel. You just need to step back and examine how you're living your life. You need to look closely at every hour of your day to see what patterns you've been forming through the years.

Do you start your morning with a high-glycemic juice and a bowl of refined cereal? Or do you miss breakfast because you're on the road? Decisions like this literally form the way your day is going, and they have a major effect on your moods, your energy levels, your thought, and, of course, your weight.

We all know the old-fashioned saying: "You didn't gain weight or grow your unhealthful habits overnight, so it's going to take little time to change them ...". Even though we might know it, we don't like to hear that we can't get the new body that we want today or tomorrow.

So, let's look back at what we really need to be trying to do.

Starting a diet and exercise program is a safe lifestyle choice. Making an effort to become fit is something more than just helping you to lose weight. By choosing to be fit and safe, you're telling yourself that you deserve better and want to enjoy all the benefits that come with that.

Weight loss success may or may not come overnight for you, but the crucial thing to bear in mind is that you have set yourself up to live a better quality and potentially longer life because of your decision to make a change. And yes, if you adopt the right program, you'll probably lose all the weight you want in the end.

Your "mindset" will decide how you're living your life. It's a predetermined mental attitude or predisposition, how you think about things, and it dictates how you behave. It's all unconscious, an inner file cabinet of thoughts and emotions. It will decide whether you're going to be able to break a habit and fulfill your dreams.

What to do When You Think Those Pies and Cakes Taste So Good

Ask someone who's trying to lose weight why they're eating those sweet rolls, bread loaves, and sugar cookies. They use them, of course, to supposedly comfort themselves, but many people just think that these foods taste good. Have you felt that you could be programmed to believe that it's a mindset, often called a predilection or an addiction? Do you know that the major bakeries condition your taste buds so that they can whip up and add sugar to their profits? Do you know why some people don't think these foods taste good at all? They are programmed to think that these foods are too sweet and chewy and to observe that the food makes them feel less balanced and less successful in their lives. That's the way you think, and you can change yourself if you know that you have a choice. You can tell yourself, "I don't need that extremely sugary stuff. They're unhealthful and not what I want for my life." You can then pick something else to eat that will support your life. It's not that easy to do; however, it can be achieved.

What to Do When You Think Your Habits are Comforting You

A lot of smokers, opioid users, or diet abusers think they're going to Cloud 9 when they consume the product of their choosing. Their body-minds have become used to the product, and people think that life is just perfect when they can eat or inhale or somehow drink whatever they call their "mate" of the moment. When people break out of their inner "trance" and see the habit as the opposite of a friend, a real marauder posing as a supporter, they will begin to change their relationship to that food or substance. "Look at the flower, but be the snake underneath it's what John Milton said about Satan in his epic poem, Paradise Lost. That's what these so-called "mates" are often like. The ability to see this with open eyes presents itself to us on a daily basis. "No, I don't want that. It hurts my existence," is something you can say to yourself when you invoke your power and choose your "mates".

What You Can Do to Make Wise Choices

Learn about what foods and substances do inside your body and mind.

Do some reading and research, and really consider the effects of feeding and nutrition.

Learn about what habits do to your life.

Pay attention to the effects of eating a sugary and salty snack or taking medicine. Learn what you can.

Find alternatives that you love.

Look for things that not only taste good and feel good, but are good for you as well.

Learn more about the food system.

See how built-in patterns are shaped in the way companies prepare their food and drugs.

Look for the "I've had it" moment.

Get an idea if you're done with a habit and whether you're ready to move on.

Cleanse your body and mind.

Clean out the old food and the substances and turn over a new leaf.

Know that you deserve a lot more.

In every way, you deserve the highest and best treatment.

Speak differently to yourself.

When your inner voice prompts you to do something that is not in your best interest, say, "No. Instead, I'm doing something better for my life." Then you're going to change your decision.

Be grateful for everything you have, and better will come to you.

Your gratitude moves your mind to a higher frequency and makes your life easier.

Shift the "trance."

Wake up to a new self. You may hypnotize yourself to take the high road. You deserve the best of all! It can take more than one or two tries, but you can do it if you're willing. The "light bulb" needs to turn. The illuminated moment is now.

How Your Mindset Affects Weight Loss

Does the idea of losing weight bother you? Do you think it's hard to give up the extra cream streak of Chinese? Are you one of those who tried all kinds of exercise regimens but couldn't stick to one after three days?

Then you need to know that, with the right amount of dedication and hard work, the poorest of people and the fattest of the fat are able to lose weight and maintain a healthier lifestyle.

Overweight people tend to overeat, which means that they consume high-calorie food even though they're not especially hungry. Most of the time, they feel good about it, because consuming such delicious food isn't illegal to them. Truth be told, consuming tasty food isn't wrong, but there's a limit to everything.

Ask yourself if you still need some more complex carbs inside you. Instead of making white rice and white bread, turn to brown variants of the same. Substitute the coke and alcohol with fresh fruit juice and soups. Eat enough fiber to keep you satisfied for a longer time and eliminate the toxins from your body system at the same time.

Overweight people not only need to decrease their calorie consumption, they also need to burn more calories than they eat on a regular basis. Otherwise, they will be able to regulate weight gain, but it will not be possible to lose the already existing fat. This involves serious exercise routines.

If you think you can substitute a good old tried and true method of sweating it out in the gym with some "100 percent pure" fat-reducing pill, then you're wrong. Nothing works better than a healthy diet combined with daily exercise.

Make sure that you combine exercise and weight training in your exercise routine. Exercise helps you burn calories rapidly and increases blood circulation. Weight training removes muscle fat very rapidly. The right proportion of both will help you lose weight effectively. Remember one thing: even if you hit your target weight after practicing this lifestyle, don't go back to your binging habits and laziness, otherwise all the lost weight will be regained again.

Weight loss, therefore, involves a change in the individual's everyday habits, and this requires a lot of strength of will.

Giving up smoking and alcohol consumption is highly advisable. Make sure you are not over-stuffed whenever you eat a meal. Always eat less than the maximum capacity you have. Avoid taking the dessert's second servings. Finally, do not crash diet, because this only has temporary outcomes.

Learning to Love Your Body

In order to be smaller, twenty-four percent of women and seventeen percent of men state that they will give up more than three years of life. That's according to a poll conducted by the magazine Psychology Today.

Studies show, at the same time, that half of American women overestimatethe magnitude of their bodies. The problem is attributed to a variety of factors, including media and cultural factors, by sociologists studying the Western world phenomenon of poor body image. Both parental and peer influences play a role as well.

The advertising industry links materialism with the already complicated question of body image. Capital, health, and beauty are correlated with a slender body, while sloth, indulgence, and a lack of self-control are associated with a heavier body. The influence of the media and society can be enhanced by psychological factors. Girls who witness sexual violence or experience an emotionally taxing puberty are more vulnerable to body dissatisfaction as adults. Women who believe they have no power over their lives are like that.

Women who have felt the most brutal blows from negative body image argue that it is not a single cause that works in isolation. A mixture of factors, such as a non-supportive family environment and a weak self-image, snowballed in the midst of cultural pressures, says Jennifer Tracy, who fought bulimia for nine years.

"It wouldn't matter what a model looked like if I had respect for myself or respect from my family," Tracy says, "And it wouldn't affect my personal self-esteem."

The Dangers of Body Dissatisfaction

We motivate ourselves to address the issue when we understand that it is a mix of factors that contribute to body dissatisfaction. By breaking the chain of these forces everywhere we can, we can capture power.

Carolyn Strauss, author of Specialty Photography, and a widely known authority on body image concerns, from fashion to self-esteem, is a top plus-size model. Her contributions now include her own line of apparel featured on the Home Shopping Network. She helps other women shift towards a healthier body image through it all. Strauss says the greatest chance of a negative picture of the body lies in the energy given away.

When a woman had a bad body image, she may try to find affirmation from outside to lift her spirits. The next fashion fad, the next diet, the next boyfriend, or anything but where she is now is going to be her thoughts. She can find herself living for "when I look better," Strauss says, instead of living in the moment. Note, the aim of most advertisements is to make you

'Not OK' so that you can become OK after using that product. I say,start OK, and then you'll just buy for yourself what you want to have.

Most of us can think of a period when we felt things would turn around for us with a fresh haircut, diet, or lipstick, but a lot of time and resource wastage can contribute to that mentality. Your vitality can also be depleted by excessive self-monitoring, and it can also lead to depression and aggression.

The University of Toronto published research that found that women who were interviewed after seeing magazine commercials featuring female models experienced a substantial and immediate decline in self-esteem.

Having a bad image of your body can lead to crash dieting and heavy exercise, which can lead in turn to poor eating, accidents, and depression. A negative body image can fuel an eating disorder, or Body Dysmorphic Disorder (BDD), in its most dangerous form.

The energy of your mind, spirit, and body is diverted from more salient endeavors when you are constantly distracted by physical appearance.

Solutions

Seek support.

Try to speak to a therapist or counselor if you believe your body image has become a preoccupation. Research on women and body confidence has been performed by Amoreena Brewton, a mother with a background in sociology and therapy. She says, "Some people are too deeply embedded in their problems with their bodies to fix them on their own."

Sometimes, when a person has problems, there are personal or family problems at hand.

When it comes to an eating disorder, it's strongly advisable to seek professional support.

Tracy is agreement. "In the end, my progress came from the intense desire to quit, which had been within me for years, and then with an eating disorder counselor to get into serious therapy. It was a true lifesaver to have someone working on just that area."

Make minor changes.

A global shift in cultural and economic systems would no doubt help us all to achieve a more positive picture of the body. "But supermodels, compensated endorsements, and the unstoppable" race for the greatest "bandwagon will probably still be there.

Enforce improvements on a smaller scale instead. Brewton recommends that we avoid allowing our lives to have such negative powers. "Buy Redbook, don't buy Cosmo," she says. Look at very powerful, smart, successful women whom you admire as much as you can. For instance, Oprah, Rosie, Hillary, Martha, your aunt, your daughter, or your grandmother can be an image you want to see.

Use positive affirmations.

Do not let your mindset get lost in negativity when you find yourself commiserating about tight blue jeans. Follow it with ten positive thoughts when the negative voice appears. Tracy says the secret is repetition. "It starts with the re-recording
22

ofthe negative messages that are so painful in your own mind," she says. About 500,000 times, I've probably re-recorded the post, and I keep losing it. But it's easier to find it, only for the next time.

Remember your spiritual connection.

Strauss says, "The first thing to note is that the world does not make mistakes." There is a reason why you are where you are. Recognize this and then choose how to continue with the next minute of your life, hour, day.

For the religious and spiritual among us, your body image will quickly improve with the simple reminder that God created you with the body you have for a reason. He didn't make you look like Cindy Crawford because you're not Cindy Crawford. He wants you to be strong and healthy enough to do the job of your life. To live and work at the optimum level. So, embrace and cultivate His development.

Surround yourself with supportive friends.

Tracy says, "When I started to heal from bulimia little by little, I didn't surround myself with people who were concentrated on body size." I position myself among the beautiful, powerful, and intelligent women who really put little focus on looks.

Brewton often recommends surrounding yourself with friends whose attention is not on strangers. "By being leaders and leading by example, other women will make the greatest difference in our lives," says Brewton. She proposes that we find a community of people.

Women frequently meet to address topics that are important to our lives; however, she notes, must concentrate primarily on body problems. "As a group, obsessing as a group is no better than obsessing as a group."

Either in your community or online, find a group of supportive women and then use this healthy, non-critical space to motivate one another.

Focus on health.

Change your relationship with food. Food is an active living fuel. Do not aim for a number on the scale, but for a weight at which you feel strong and energetic. Ask yourself if your health and energy levels contribute to or take away from your diet.

Our bodies have a simpler time finding our optimum weight when we avoid concentrating on our bodies and start focusing on our wellbeing instead.

Those who do this are more than twice as likely to lose weight as people who are less prepared to feel happier with their bodies.

We can control how much influence food has over us, Tracy proves. "In my success, one of the most significant factors are eating whatever and whatever I want, whenever. I don't in any way diet, limit, or make rules for myself. This sets up my life so that I feel less limited and needy for food. For me, it has taken a lot of significance out of food," says Tracy. "I've lost fifteen pounds since I left my bulimic conduct, my face and cheeks aren't bloated, and I feel very good at it."

Change your relationship with exercise.

Regular exercise generates strength and stamina, which will allow you to enjoy more sports. Are you able to hike as far as you like? Do you want to try kayaking? Do you know the joys of a "runner's high"? Find a workout you love. If you hate aerobic dancing, don't think about it taking a lesson in aerobics. Do not consider going to the gym if you hate it. Instead, experiment with movements that you've never done before. Is there any exercise that makes you feel motivated physically? Just do that one.

By reminding yourself of the blast of energy that immediately accompanies a workout, you will inspire yourself to practice.

Change your relationship with your body.

Your body is a tool for your mind when food becomes a tool for active living, and exercise becomes a tool for enhanced strength. Your body instantly has stamina,and the courage to do what the mind wants. "Our bodies are miracles, walking in the skin around us," says Brewton. You are never going to see a finer piece of art or machinery.

"Imagine for a second if you took all the time you spend worrying about beauty and concentrate on how much you enjoy your ability to interact well, or what a wonderful mom you are, or ways to address the issue of homelessness," Brewton says. "If you took if negative energy and used it for good, not only will your life and life be good.".

You might just be disappointed if you want to learn the secrets of weight loss. It may seem that everyone you know has found out how to lose weight, but somehow you keep missing the point. You may have tried diet after diet, you may have bought a dozen items for weight loss, or you may have dabbled in exercise without visible results.

We live in a generation expecting quick fulfillment. We plan to miss a meal or two and see a difference on the scale. We believe we should be able to shop for smaller clothing after a week at the gym.

The basic thing you need to do to do the secrets of weight loss is to be careful with the process. It didn't take a day or two, or even a month or two, to become overweight. If you travel 100 miles out of your way through the woods, you're not going to find your way back by walking a mile. You have to take your time and trust that this has been done by others, and you can also too. If you're middle-aged, you're a mile-old.

Over time, minor changes can make a world of difference, changes such as taking the stairs instead of the elevator, parking at the far end of the parking lot, and preferring water over soda. Later, greater changes, such as watching fat content and joining a gym, can be added to the minor changes you began with.

It's a secret that has the power to change your life completely, particularly once you know how to apply it, and it's a secret that is so simple that it stays concealed from view for most people. However, you will feel some different emotions once you discover this secret. You're going to feel let down because it's not some exotic, magical cure that's going to make all your extra pounds melt away.

Let me warn you again about the feelings that you will feel when I share this secret. The trick to handling these feelings is to realize how to apply the secret to your own personal life. I'm going to help you do that, but you have to continue reading the rest of the book. In the following formula, the secret to weight loss is found:

Calories In against Calories Out = Weight Gain, Weight Loss or Weight Remains the Same.

The formula is that simple and how to apply the formula is the key to weight loss. " Calories In" represents the calories you absorb into your body via the foods you consume and the beverages you drink. "Calories Out" simply means the calories your body burns depending on the metabolism and the activities you take part in. If the "Calories In" is much more than the "Calories Out", you will benefit less from the "Calories Out".

Application of the Secret to Weight Loss

You should go through rigorous testing to assess your basal metabolism and how many calories your body burns every day. To evaluate the number of calories you eat on a daily basis, you could have someone examine your food consumption, but there are simpler ways to determine where you are in the scale challenge. Just ask yourself this question: "Has my weight stayed the same?" Your response will demonstrate what you need to do in the sense of weight loss.

If your weight has stayed the same for the last four weeks, your intake of "Calories In" is equal to your expenditure of "Calories Out." If your core goal is losing weight, then the implementation of this formula is extremely effective because you have three weight-loss strategies:

- Method 1-Decrease your calorie consumption!
- Method 2-Increase your spending on calories!
- Method 3-Do the two!

In just a minute, we will explore these strategies in more detail. But first, we need to answer those who have seen their weight rise over the last four weeks. Let's say over the last four weeks you have seen a 2-pound weight gain. In a pound of fat, there are 3,500 calories. You can measure (on average) how many extra calories you eat over the amount you burn on a daily basis by using the following formula.

No pounds gained: 3500 times divided by 28 days is equivalent to additional calories per day.

2 x 3500 divided by 28 = 250 daily calories

You eat 250 more calories per day than you burn up from your metabolism and activities, by using the above example for this formula. If you were to use Approach 1, you would need to reduce your caloric intake by 250 calories in order to prevent weight gain. If you followed Method 2, then to avoid the weight gain, you will need to raise your activity level by 250 calories. Alternatively, you might use a mixture of Strategies 1 & 2 to remove the extra 250 calories each day to keep your weight steady.

Method 1 - Reduce Your Caloric Intake!

Method 1 is the simplest and best way to execute your weight loss program. Method 1 doesn't have to be a severe caloric restriction program. Remember, you most likely didn't immediately gain all your weight, but did so over a period of time. So, look at each of your meals to get rid of 50 to 100 calories. Some suggestions are listed here:

- The most effective move that you can take is this: turn from soda to water. There are 140-150 calories in a 12 oz soft drink, and water has none! 1.5 cans of soda are consumed every day by the average American. It will save them 230 calories a day by moving to water. Don't make the mistake of switching to diet pop! Diet pops do not reduce thirst. Hunger is not eliminated by diet pops. Water does that! Plus, the liver uses a lot of the water in diet pop to help it eliminate toxins, but none of it goes to the cells. In a detrimental way, this affects metabolism.

- Split those spreads in half. 100 calories are one ounce of butter or cream cheese. Cut the portion you usually use in half; if you've only saved 50 calories or less, then turn to an alternative if you don't want to cut the number. You could use the Smart Balance Light Butter Spread at 47 calories per ounce instead of butter. Switch to Sugar-Free if you use jam on your bread each day. You're going to go from 50 calories to 10 and save 40 calories for yourself.

- Seek alternatives. To save 50 calories, try tomatoes and mustard instead of mayonnaise. For 65-calorie savings plus required fiber, consider an apple or pear at 90 calories rather than of a vending size of a bag of potato chips at 155 calories. Substitute a low-fat dressing instead of a high-fat creamy dressing to save 80 to 150 calories. It'll save you 80 calories by selecting a grilled piece of meat instead of a breaded, deep-fried piece of meat.

- Reduce the size of the portions. If you like French Fries, then select the small size at 210 calories versus the medium at 450 calories or the large size at 540 calories, depending on your preference, to save 90 to 330 calories. Take half of your eatery meal home in a "doggy bag" because many restaurant meals max out at 1700 calories or more. Avoid eating "Super Size" meals because all they do is make you "Mega-Sized"! If you don't feed your dog, then the next day, you have a meal that saves you both calories and money. Go for a 6-ounce glass of juice instead of a 12-ounce glass of juice and save yourself 85 calories.

Method 2 - Increase Your Caloric Expenditure!

The key way to raise your caloric expenditure is to exercise, but it will not have the same effect on weight loss as Method 1. I know that there are a lot of exercisers who disagree with me, but here are the cold hard facts. Take an average individual weighing 175 lbs. About 250 calories will be expended on working out at a moderate pace for 30 minutes. Note that the French Fries order is small in size at 210 calories. It doesn't take you 30 minutes to eat those French Fries. In weight control, exercise is necessary, but it is more critical for your overall general health. Consider things that automatically lead to your calorie expenditure, such as:

- Play with the children. It will not only build a special bond but, for 30 minutes, light to moderate play will burn 111 to 159 calories for 175 lbs.

- Sitting up rather than lying down. Only shifting your place from lying on the couch to sitting up will help you burn about 60 more calories per hour.

- Choose purposefully to spend more calories. Instead of identifying the nearest parking space, park instead at the back of the parking lot and walk further to the front door. Take the stairs rather than the elevator to go to the second or third floor. Wash your car yourself instead of making someone elsedo it at the car wash. Do some general cleaning instead of making the dust accumulate around the house. During the day, all these additional exercises will help you consume an extra 100 calories.

- Find an activity that you enjoy. Depending on your weight and strength, 30 minutes could burn anywhere from 100 to 250 calories, whether it's spent on a leisurely bike ride, a bowling party, general exercise, basketball, soccer, gardening, playing a musical instrument, or some other sport.

- Drink water. In order to increase your stamina and general metabolism, just this easy exercise can do wonders. This will assist you during the day to burn more calories.

Method 3-Do Both

This is the true secret to weight management since it helps to drive a more productive weight loss program and weight management lifestyle on both sides of the equation. It will have a beneficial effect on your overall general health and will lead to the slowing down of the aging process.

CHAPTER TWO

SELF HYPNOSIS AND WEIGHT LOSS

Everyone has that one food weakness that they just don't seem to be able to stop. It might be buttery popcorn or salty chips, or it might be some sort of sweet, like soda, chocolate, or ice cream. It is possible that whatever your food vice is, it is one big factor that is holding you back from your overall goals of weight loss. However, the good news is that the food you choose is definitely not the biggest problem. It's how you treat food, that's the problem. While sweets should certainly not be part of your regular meal schedule, when losing weight, you can still eat the foods you love: you just need to do it consciously.

That's where hypnosis, or, more precisely, clinical hypnotherapy, comes in. You learn to retrain your mind with hypnosis, to obtain a new outlook on the foods you consume. You have a better chance of actually kicking your addiction to mindless snacking when you can change your mindset towards food so that you can get healthier in the long term.

Train Yourself to Enforce the Barrier Effect

We do so in ways that set us up to overindulge as most of us reach for our favorite snacks. We grab the chips from the party-sized bag, the full pint of ice cream (and a spoon), or whatever other food item we want, and just dive in. The issue with this is that whenever you eat this way, there is no calorie liability and this lack of portion control, or the absence of a barrier, is a major part of the process when it comes to healthy eating. In fact, researchers have shown that we consume 40 percent of our food when we eat directly from the source than if we portion our food.

So, it's necessary to portion out your food to prevent this mindless feeding. You can retrain your mind via hypnosis so that you can still offer yourself a barrier or a stopping point when you are going to plate up your food, whether it's at mealtime or snack time. With portion control in place, you force yourself to consider whether you really want another bag or bowl value-consciously and intentionally.

Train Yourself to Stop Once the Food No Longer Tastes as Good as It Initially Did

You can learn to listen to your body with hypnosis so that you know when you've had enough to feel fulfilled without overeating. A way to do this is to train your mind to want to stop eating when your meal no longer tastes as good as it was at the very first bite.

For starters, it's a very rewarding experience when you've had ice cream for the first time in a long while. It's cold and nice, and your serotonin flows, and it feels amazing! But this feeling is going to begin to wear off reasonably quickly. You'll find that when you've equipped your brain with weight loss hypnosis, you don't really need to hit the bottom of the bowl for your craving to be fulfilled.

These tricks are deceptively simple, but they are highly efficient ways to resist the urge to eat mindlessly so that you lose weight and keep it off.

Determination to Lose Weight

Are you determined to lose weight? You want to prevent the complications of heart disease, diabetes, and elevated cholesterol levels that are associated with being overweight for most individuals, including yourself. However, because of their fitness, not everyone goes on a quest to lose weight. You can want to lose weight because you see weight loss as a way to make others look desirable and improve your self-image. In order to recover your usual body weight, there are several preventive steps you might take. People around the world spend thousands and even millions of dollars annually on losing weight by attempting these steps. Exercise gadgets, healthier organic foods, dietary supplements, slimming pills, diets, and fitness clubs are spent on these vast amounts of money every day.

Simply put, weight loss is a multimillion-dollar business. Are you still going to lose weight with these measures? No, I still believe the answer may be yours. The actual response may sound pretty simplistic to you, but it is real. That simple little secret of weight loss is the magic response. You must change the way you think about yourself and food. Take this case: do you recall those times, when you were on that expensive wonder diet, that you watched your weight rigorously but still struggled to keep your eyes off that creamy dessert after meals or didn't even feel bold enough to cut off your craving for chocolate?

Hold on to this condition for a while, and I will explain further why, considering your rigorous workout routine, diet classes, and the slimming pills, you are struggling to keep your weight down.

It may not be as easy for you to believe, but I can assure you that the reason you feel you're losing the war is easy. The explanation is that you have not changed the habits of your old thoughts about how you felt about the creamy dessert and the chocolate bar and, more importantly, about yourself. This example is to show you that your weight loss can be influenced by your thinking patterns.

As human beings, our emotions and beliefs affect our actions, which then cause us to respond in a certain way to a situation. The little thoughts you used to have about the beautiful dessert or chocolate afteryour meals would have prompted you to choose to skip the dessert, or to just take a bite and then finish it all. Unfortunately, your above intervention will be to the detriment of your effort at losing any weight.

You may also regulate your emotions, on the other hand, or make suggestions in your mind to alter how you feel about the dessert and chocolate. The good news is that you can control your emotions or make suggestions to your mind on how you react to the dessert or the pudding without weakening your weight loss program. Hypnosis will show you how you can make these suggestions to control the emotions in the head.

Hypnosis is an interaction between yourself and the hypnotist. A hypnotist is someone who is trained to use hypnotic methods or therapy and is skilled. The hypnotist will attempt to manipulate or make suggestions on your thoughts and behavior during this interaction by specifically focusing on ideas and images that may elicit any expected results verbally.

You can receive advice from the hypnotist to lose weight through hypnosis that will change your previous emotions or perceptions about the factors that could have contributed to your weight gain. You may also opt not to see the hypnotist face to face when you chose to use hypnosis.

In addition to this being the overview of the mechanism of helping to facilitate progress, it also happens to be a mechanism that many of us have found works naturally. Some of us have come upon the process of programming our minds with the ambitions and accomplishments and milestones we aspire to, and have been able to proceed and accomplish them.

Planning for success

So now that you have a clear understanding of what hypnosis is, you can see that helps our mind function in its most efficient way to accomplish any objective. We first have to imagine what the aim is in order to achieve a target. In order to get closer to our target, we have to prepare for what steps to take. That's the first step: the awareness of what the purpose is. Once you have that in mind, you then build an overview of how to get there. It could be one method that leads you to the end goal all the way, or it could be several that lead you along the way to the end goal via intermediate objectives.

How self-hypnosis for weight loss works.

Now that you put this together for weight loss, you must mentally plan to lose weight first: perhaps in percentages, perhaps focusing on a specific dress size you want to fit into, or perhaps you have a precise weight in mind. It would be very simple to use self-hypnosis for weight loss at this stage. Using self-hypnosis to enhance the motivation to lose weight, you will visualize life at your desired weight when in a self-induced hypnotic trance. Imagine wearing the same size of dress yourself and begin to imagine all the advantages of wearing that dress: what it looks like, how you look in the mirror, how people react to you, and so on. What you want to do is trigger all the good feelings that fuel the drive to lose weight.

Using your mind to rehearse behavior makes it familiar.

So, is weight loss self-hypnosis a fraud? Well, you're fooling yourself if you think that, by putting yourself in a trance, that the fat would simply melt off you without modifying any of your acts. If anyone tells you that their product is going to do that, I'd suggest that you're probably being fooled. With that said, it may seem as if you're only doing what you normally do every day when you change your mind, mood, and desires, but you've changed your actions enough that weight appears to melt away from you magically.

Since self-hypnosis is not going to magically make you melt fat, you know there are concrete steps that are required to lose weight. These behaviors typically include eating less and bringing more exercise or movement into your life. So, the next move will be using your self-hypnosis trance to visualize yourself doing whatever action you have wanted to do to help you lose weight. You might use your imagination to picture eating less, leaving food on your plate, taking smaller quantities, eating less frequently, etc., if you wanted to consume less food. Every time you use your imagination to behave this way, you incorporate the emotional feeling of pleasure, happiness, and all of the feelings previously encountered to enhance your weight loss desire.

What you are doing is connecting acts to positive emotions that will help you to stay on track with your weight loss program. If you believed that weight loss self-hypnosis meant that you would magically melt fat off your body without any behavioral adjustments, then you misunderstood what weight loss self-hypnosis was about. Self-hypnosis for weight loss is an efficient way to make things happen by programming your mind to take on new habits instead of just repeating what you are used to doing in order to gain what you really want.

The advantages of self-hypnosis are essentially infinite. Each person is special and, under hypnosis, reacts differently. The advantages of self-hypnosis reaped by a person can, therefore, differ. It also relies on what effects you expect to obtain from hypnosis and how far you want to go.

Many use self-hypnosis over the years to boost their memory, lose weight, accomplish goals, and gain trust in themselves. I would like to point out that self-hypnosis is not a magic pill. The improvements that you foresee will not happen overnight. Despite this, it sure makes it simple and fun to adjust. It's like a supporting tool to help you make those desired improvements to your life.

In sports, a coach helps you make your game easier. However, even the most specialized coach in the world can't support you if you don't put in the time and practice. In the end, to be a better player, you must make it a point to work on your game. To become a better sportsperson, you have to shape certain behaviors and develop certain attitudes.

In the same way, what self-hypnosis does is to direct you to develop those values, attitudes, habits, and behaviors that, at a subconscious level, can trigger successful changes, which will further contribute to the desired outcomes that you want to achieve.

The essential benefits of self-hypnosis are the development and formation of supportive attitudes and behaviors that will contribute to the desired improvements.

Let's look at the essential advantages of self-hypnosis:

Stress Management and Relaxation.

No matter whether you think self-hypnosis works for you or not, you will certainly enjoy being comfortable when in a trance. It is a relief if there is any tangible advantage that you can obtain from hypnosis. Your mind and body are totally relaxed while you are under hypnosis. Relaxation in itself is very effective in avoiding stress-related diseases in today's world that we face.

When you are comfortable under hypnosis:

- The heart continues to relax and slows down to its normal pace.

- It lowers blood pressure.

- All your tissues and organs have an adequate supply of blood.

- Respiration slows down, reducing the need for oxygen.

All of the above later leads to improved control of stress and anxiety, enhanced creativity, a feeling of relaxation, and stronger concentration. The brain also triggers the release of endorphins in your body, contributing to a sense of pleasure and well-being.

Depression.

Depression is a learned trait in the majority of situations. There are only a few individuals whose genetic makeup might make them easy prey to depression. You can catch the flu and cold, but you can't catch depression. To become depressed actually needs effort on your part. To feel sad, you must think of suicidal thoughts continuously. Depression sufferers sound depressed, act depressed, and act in ways that will help their depression.

Research has found that constant negative thoughts and actions contribute to certain changes in the brain's nervous system. Later, this leads to physical symptoms such as headaches, aches in the body, and ulcers. It can lead to suicidal thoughts and psychiatric illnesses in severe cases of persistent depression.

One of the benefits of self-hypnosis is that it allows you to unlearn and hold off thinking habits and behaviors that add to depression. It makes you shift your life perspective from feeling sad to feeling amazing.

Habits Formation.

Habits are learned. As a human, you are a creature of habit. Most of your life is managed by the routines you have created, and habits let you move on with your life with the least amount of mental effort on the part of your brain.

Just imagine if you didn't have any routines, and everything you did was new to you. You'd end up wasting a lot of your mental and physical resources by performing regular activities consciously. This would be stressful and time-consuming.

For instance, think of driving to work: if every day was like the first day you began learning to drive, how would you navigate traffic?

A very important advantage of self-hypnosis is habit development. You can develop positive habits and unlearn poor ones through the use of self-hypnosis. Among the common bad habits that can be resolved with self-hypnosis are smoking, nail-biting, bedwetting, and eating disorders.

Fears and Phobias.

The brain does not differentiate between actual events and imaginary ones. A phobia or a fear is an unfounded danger to one's own imagination, both are rooted in the brain within the amygdala. As a child, you are born with just two kinds of fear: heights and loud noises. When you get older, all other kinds of fears are developed, but they are nothing but the response of your brain to protect you. Your brain's optimistic purpose of defending and safeguarding you is behind all fears.

One of the most sought-after advantages of self-hypnosis is eradicating irrational fears and learning to cope successfully with phobias.

Overcoming Addictions.

Overcoming addictions is another advantage of self-hypnosis. Self-hypnosis is not enough in itself to overcome addictions, though. In combination with Cognitive Behavioral Therapy (CBT), it is claimed that addictions have been quickly resolved and permanently put off.

Addictions are reliance on an external stimulus, substance, or a habit that, with one's choice, may not be prevented. This is the distinction between behaviors and addictions as well. Unlike behaviors, until you have sufficient therapeutic assistance, you cannot control addictions.

Alcoholism, drugs, gambling, sex, and smoking are all common forms of addiction.

Performance Enhancement.

Your success or failure might depend more on the beliefs in your mind that you create. You must have good supportive values to boost your chances of success in whatever area you chose.

Be a better salesperson, a better runner, better speaker, lose or gain weigh,t or something you want to work on if you want to enhance your game. First, you have to begin with the confidence that it's possible, and you can accomplish it. However, it's usually not as direct as it seems. We set limits on what we are and are not capable of due to past conditioning, disappointments, adverse climates, and negative experiences in life. Mostly, our inner critic or aware mind sets these limits. You skip the conscious mind instantly in self-hypnosis and deal with that part of your subconscious mind that is capable of making our goals come true.

You may overcome these psychological obstacles or self-sabotages with self-hypnosis and go full out and accomplish those objectives.

However, if you want to lose a few pounds and you think that this target is far from feasible in this life because of the drastic changes that it needs from you, try to rethink. Despite these methods being in existence for a long time now, when you want to make this purpose a reality, there is still a need for the most skilled and greatest help. There are several hypnotherapy CDs on the market at the moment for weight loss. Therefore, you can easily get these audio hypnosis therapy tools if you need to burn the extra weight off your system and become a happier person. It has been thought that, if you can use other CDs efficiently, a dieter might possibly correct her or his habit patterns completely in just one or two lessons. The audio disc was specifically produced to provide brilliant effects on the way of thinking of a person as it begins to respond to self-hypnosis of fat loss and also to go along with the healthy routine immediately. These forms of self-hypnosis do not last for years, unlike many diets on the market; this method, in fact, could last for a lifetime. You can permanently lose weight quickly; your mind has become ready to do all the things that can help you maintain the size you want.

First, every week you may need to be present in a session and also listen to a hypnosis CD about how to rapidly shed mass for around twenty minutes each and every day. This is very good for relieving you of problems with the newest as well as your former way of life, which will thus give you a greater approach to your routine. The results of the method will vary in terms of time, but on average, one would certainly be able to lose about 4kg of weight in just twenty-eight days. Just in case you shed the extra kilos fast and steadily, adjusting to the changes would be less difficult for your body system, and it is the main reason why the effects come to be long-term.

Therefore, if you are struggling to have the opportunity to lose weight quickly by weight loss hypnosis, then you can be confident that these CDs or DVDs can do wonders along with daily sessions with a therapist. In promoting your entire life, both of these healthy times are definitely important because you are able to start having control over your responses, thereby allowing you to be happier and better in terms of making decisions about being physically fit.

Many individuals have either heard of hypnosis or have witnessed hypnotization of others. Self-hypnosis does not suggest that a person is sitting in a trance without regulating what they do or say. Instead, this means being in complete control of one's subconscious mind. For the purpose of reprogramming their desires as well as their inner belief structure, one bypasses their conscious mind by self-hypnosis techniques. They increase the chances of changing their lives positively when one deals with their subconscious mind.

Self-hypnosis can be of extreme benefit across diverse techniques. One can achieve sharper concentration, beat addictions, strengthen relationships, enhance wellness, achieve success, and so on. In reality, because of these advantages, major companies and businesses also use self-hypnosis to maximize productivity for their workers. Using binaural beats that work with brain frequencies to allow a person to tap into their subconscious mind and work with various altered states of mind is one of the best and most accessible methods for self-hypnosis. The mind attains a high concentration when one listens to binaural beats, which enables a person to respond quickly to instructions.

Naturally, when it removes negative factors, the human mind has the potential to respond to positive aspects. Not only does the successful use of binaural beats offer outstanding results, but these effects are long-term as well. In addition, binaural beats not only encourage a person to achieve their goals, but also enable one to increase their memory, gain a sharper focus on the mind, and achieve much greater self-confidence. In reality, self-hypnosis using binaural beats can positively alter a person's way of approaching life.

In fact, it is believed that binaural beats are the quickest and easiest way one can use to achieve great success. Notice that this procedure, which is one of the methods of brainwave training that has been around for some years, has been scientifically proven. There is also no reason why it should not be used by an individual to attain success in their lives. Each person has goals that they want to accomplish, such as a career, relationships, health, and so on. It is much simpler to accomplish these goals by using binaural beats and other brainwave training techniques.

In addition to general relaxation, listening to binaural beats helps a person to easily fall asleep, in addition to enjoying a deeper and more restful sleep. Binaural beats, among other self-hypnosis techniques, are known to enable a person to achieve very deep meditation stages. This is because binaural beats allow one to feel low frequencies of brainwave, which are connected to high levels of awareness and deeper meditation. As they are able to relax the mind and body, binaural beats also aid in reducing tension. They also help one to think clearly, helping a person to cope with stress in a better way. There are some frequencies that have been demonstrated to assist the body of a person to recover rapidly and strengthen their immune system as well as relieve pain. There is no reason why the use of binaural beats should be left to companies and athletes over other individuals only with these advantages in mind.

Although most people would equate hypnosis with a person sitting comfortably in the office of a hypnotherapist, there are many methods that can be learned by self-hypnosis and applied to yourself. It's possible for you to gain full mastery of your mind, including the subconscious, through these techniques. In this book, we will cover the key strategies that you can adapt and modify to suit your own needs. It should be noted that caution should be taken when determining what you want to get programmed into your subconscious mind.

The basic thing to do is determine what your hypnosis session's desired outcome or intention would be. During a session, you should not try to alter more than one thing, as it simply will not work. It is time to formulate the statement or suggestion you are going to send to your subconscious mind once you have decided on your intent.

The suggestions you give to your subconscious during self-hypnosis require a great deal of thought. They need to be hopeful, a positive improvement, or something good, and reflect this. Using a harmful suggestion will only help to intensify a fear, for example telling yourself "I will fly across the country no matter how scared I am". Instead, reflect more on the good things involved in traveling and how you will feel when you get to your destination and your loved ones welcome you. It should be brief and to the point, and quickly recall the ideas you formulate.

Do it in a quiet, calm, and relaxed position when you are ready to do a self-hypnosis session. To make sure you are not interrupted, locking the doors and unplugging the phone will help. As long as your body is totally relaxed and able to settle along with your mind, you can either sit or lay down.

Focus all your attention on a point quite above the level of the eye. When saying the word "relax" to yourself, take a few deep breaths. Imagine that you are throwing out all of the bad air inside you as you breathe out and replacing it with good clean air as you breathe in. Close your eyes and concentrate on a few of the sounds around you, such as water in the pipes, the wind blowing outside through the trees, or rain hitting the walls. Be conscious of your physical body and what you feel, such as the temperature of your skin or the weight of your body against your bed or chair, at the same time.

Start to descend into your subconscious mind once you are comfortable. You can imagine walking down a short stairway to a lovely garden or some other spot that will offer you enjoyment. Each action you take takes you closer to your target, such as moving through layers of clouds and eventually leaving all your worries. You are in your garden at the bottom step and can feel the sun on the tops of your feet and the grass between your toes.

You should now be fully comfortable in both your body and your mind. Start silently repeating your ideas to yourself and your subconscious mind. Repeat the suggestion three times with a quick break in between to imagine how your life will be when the change is made. When your advice is done, move back up the stairway slowly, reminding yourself that you will be fully awake and refreshed at the top floor.

The capacity to hypnotize yourself is an ability that almost everybody can master. Training does, however, make it easier to achieve. You may not instantly notice the impact of it, but just do it again and have confidence that you can make the changes in your life that you want to makeover time by giving your subconscious mind the good suggestions.

It is pretty easy to do self-hypnosis for weight loss. Once you have got your body into a fully comfortable state, you use strategies such as visualization and constructive self-talk to program your mind to think in a new manner.

Step 1

To practice self-hypnosis for weight loss, the first thing you need to do is to get comfortable. It works best to lie down; just make sure you don't fall asleep. Start by tensing and then relaxing each part of your body from your brow down to your toes to relieve tension in your body. You can envision standing under a gentle waterfall as you're doing this and imagine that the water rushing over your body is washing away all your tension.

Step 2

Next, you'll want to concentrate on breathing. Imagine that your body fills up while you are inhaling pure, fresh oxygen. You say the word relax to yourself as you slowly exhale. You can imagine yourself slowly going down a long flight of stairs to deepen your sense of relaxation or simply count down from 100 as you concentrate on your body relaxing more and more.

Step 3

You will use constructive phrases to solve the problems surrounding you until you are absolutely comfortable. You may want to try suggestions such as "I enjoy the taste of fruit and vegetables", "I love my feelings after I exercise my body", and "I enjoy being lean and active" if you are using self-hypnosis for weight loss. You just need to keep practicing these affirmations until you feel comfortable.

Step 4

To get back to consciousness, simply count from 0 to 10 until you feel fully awake when concentrating on the numbers. You will have to count from 0 to 10 more than once before you are ready to get up and resume daily activities.

CHAPTER THREE

MINDFUL EATING HABITS

Choosing the right food is just one component of the equation when it comes to eating right. The need to follow conscientious eating habits is also crucial when deciding whether you really are hungry or to give in to emotional eating because you are depressed, sad, lonely, or bored. Many of us want to use food to ease those unpleasant emotions, and therefore take in a lot more calories than we should, perhaps without even understanding it. In addition to making you feel bad for eating it, the food also does not solve the dilemma that brought on the mood in the first place. So, you're not acquiring anything but extra weight.

Here's how the difference between feeling hungry physically and emotionally can be established.

Physical hunger goes steadily on, and the longer it's been since you last fed, the heavier it gets. You may find that you are grumpy, that you are tired, that your stomach is growling, that you have difficulty focusing or concentrating, or that you may have a headache.

Another way to detect physical hunger is to watch how you feel twenty minutes to half an hour after eating. Feeling better means that you're still hungry. Feeling the same, or even worse, indicates the eating was for emotional purposes.

Emotional appetite seems to come easily, so you feel the need to feed it right away. Possibly, you might even be feelingdesperate to get some food.

Other symptoms of emotional hunger are cravings for something very particular, eating greater quantities than normal, and then feeling guilty. Suppose your diet or snack doesn't make your bad emotions go away, and after the meal is done, you feel exactly the same. That's emotional eating.

Stop to think about whether you're physically hungry or whether you're eating for some reason while you're about to snack or go for some serving instead. Often, it's hard to know the difference. According to experts, what you need to do is to ask yourself if eating can fix your problem.

For both of us, the great news is that there are simple ways to manage emotional malnutrition. You might do other things to make you feel better and practice doing each one by thinking about them. Begin by asking yourself: "What do I feel?" Then follow that up with: "How am I going to feel better?" Food won't always be the solution.

- Try to go for a walk if you're bored, play with a per, dance to some music, any productive pursuit will do.

- If you're sad, speak to a friend you trust, or write down how you feel just for your own eyes. No one is happy every single moment; it's all right to show sorrow, feel it, and then rise.

- Try some ideas for stress control if you're depressed. Create a list of all your unfinished duties and place them in order of importance for each assignment. Create a schedule to get things done, and if the list is too much to handle, don't be afraid to ask for help.

- If you're anxious, burn off the extra nervous energy every day with hiking, biking, or some other aerobic exercise generating sweat. It always burns away the tension.

You might need a bit of practice to set mindful eating habits in motion, but after using them a few times, you can see that thought before eating gives you an opportunity to make a decision that may not feel all that easy at first, but will be very much healthier for you in the long run. It's about getting better more conveniently. You'll have such an amazing sense of power over your diet before you know it. Have you have taken care of your emotional eating rather than being governed by it?

How to Identify and OvercomeNegative Eating Habits

Food patterns — which may have been well developed since childhood — are what most people who want to lose weight generally find it hard to alter. Weight loss is also difficult since these patterns typically result in overeating, which can of course add more calories quickly.

For example, if you were always rewarded with food for being a good kid when you were young, you might continue to see food as a sign of reward or comfort as you grow older. You may have had heavy snacks at midday since you were a little kid too, so as you age it may just be hard to break that habit.

Eating in front of the television is among the most common unhealthy eating habits. This can lead to mindless eating, where even when you are full, you keep eating because you are not concentrating on the eating process, your mind being occupied by other items instead. You may have grown used to the habit of eating ice cream before sleep, too! Without you even knowing it, that can really add pounds!

Don't despair and feel as though you can't change your ways at this point. What you need to do is list some of the eating habits that you have gained over the years and evaluate which ones are bad for your weight loss program. It takes a lot of discipline to break habits that do not help you to lose weight, just like any other bad habit. Be frank with yourself after analyzing what these eating habits are and finding ways to break them one by one.

The only way to break a bad habit is to replace it with a new one. For instance, during meals, you can simply turn the TV off. When you do, you find that you can savor the food better and you can hear yourself think. Not having the television on during family meals will facilitate family talks, which will bring the family together as well. The more distractions you eliminate when eating, the more attention your mind can devote to the food you eat and to the number of calories you consume.

Here are some more thoughts that can turn your poor eating habits into good ones:

1. Remove the food from the junk. Almost all fast food, which can lead to more pounds, is rich in fat and sodium. Try yogurt or a carrot stick if you are hungry for a snack. You can also cook your own tortilla chips and make your own balanced salsa sauce. Not only is this a tastier option, but it is also a low-calorie snack.

2. Only eat if you're hungry, and not if you're frustrated, nervous, or tired. Analyze the feelings that could cause your appetite. If it is anything other than hunger, ignore the urge and do something more effective, such as walking outside or reading a book.

3. Ask the waiter to break your service into two and share it with your friend or girlfriend to avoid overeating while you're dining out. Take the remaining half in a doggie bag and consume it for your next meal if you're eating alone. As your mom tells you when you were little, you don't even need to "pick up your plate.".

Habits are patterns of action that are replicated over and over again, and we do it more subconsciously. Since eating is part of our lives, eating habits are no different. Breaking a habit is hard because, after all, it's a ritual. Keeping a positive mind and a strong resolve will help you break the habit. The real key to breaking the habit, in fact, is to keep it slow and steady. Stopping or modifying your habit gradually is how you can really break it. If you ever try to break the habit by pushing yourself to quit unexpectedly, then you're going to have a really hard time, and you may end up hurting yourself. Here are a few tips about how unhealthy eating habits can be broken.

In order to start your day, there is nothing more important to do than eating breakfast, as breakfast would be the start of breaking the habit and keeping it up during the day. Start by having a nutritious and good breakfast. Never miss breakfast because your body will go into "survival mode" if you do, slowing down your entire metabolism. This is caused by the fact that you have been sleeping for many hours and have not given your body the requisite fuel for the day. You have to stop excess fats and sugars, and instead ensure that they are balanced. For your diet, fat is essential, so don't remove it. All you need to do is take it in small quantities.

Remember to never starve yourself; the healthiest way to go is to cut back on calories because eating too little or nothing at all will hurt your health. Your cravings for fatty and sugary foods will skyrocket if you don't eat enough calories for the day, giving you an uncontrollable appetite. If you take the right amount of calories a day, let's say between 1000-1400 calories, your metabolism will not be decreased by your body. Instead, the burning of fat would also increase. Gradually decrease your calorie intake so that your body can adapt.

It can help you to break unhealthy eating habits by knowing what you eat and knowing what to avoid. Understand that drinks contain calories as well; sweet drinks in particular can have tons of calories since they're packed with sugar. Alcohol also has calories and is also a source of excess calories if you consume a lot of it. Know those small quantities of seldom eaten food can be equal to a calorie-wise meal, so strive to keep bits of sweets or candy away from you to avoid munching or nibbling.

It can also be a problem if you eat too quickly, so break this habit by starting to avoid any distractions you have while eating. Sometimes, TV, radio, or even talking while you eat will lead you to over-eating without realizing that you've eaten more than your share. Through using a smaller plate, you will break the habit. This will restrict the amount of food you place on your plate and therefore the amount of food you eat. Emotional binging is a concern, too, because many people have a propensity to eat too much when stressed. Why not try doing physical exercises instead of eating? This is better because it will also keep you occupied and make you forget about your anxiety.

Two very good descriptions of a habit are given here: a) a repeated, sometimes unconscious conduct pattern that is gained through regular repetition, and b) a developed mind or character disposition. As the description says, habits are repetitive, and your temperament, mind, and character are well defined. They are often created by repeated behavioral trends. Habits can be sweet or they can be mean. I want to concentrate on understanding and overcoming harmful eating habits in this post.

Perhaps the most difficult to break are eating habits. This is true because the development of our eating habits begins on the day we are born. They become part of the society in which we grow up. The dietary habits of the people around you are usually embraced by you as well. If you grow up in a family that eats a lot of candy or a lot of fat and greasy foods every day, and they consume a lot of it every time they eat, then you're going to follow those habits and you're going to think they're normal. The worst part of developing such habits when you grow up is that they have already been repeated enough to be firmly formed in your mind and character by the time you are old enough to recognize the risk of these eating behaviors. It is normal to feel that your shot at optimum health has been sabotaged, because, quite frankly, it has.

It will take a lot of commitment and work on your part if you want to alter your behaviors. Eating behaviors are well developed in our minds, as stated in the concept of habits. When you plan to modify your eating habits, this is the first thing to reflect on. At the mental stage, you must clearly believe that you have been eating all the wrong foods all your life. You must persuade yourself that today, not tomorrow, you must fully turn your eating habits. Then, at the internal stage, you have to reassure yourself that you are taking care of what, where, and how much you eat on a regular basis.

It is a good idea to write down what you eat, when you eat it, and how much of it you are eating to help you recognize and appreciate your poor eating habits. As most of the poor eating habits take place at the subconscious level, this is an essential exercise. We call this feeding mindless. By the time you put food in your mouth, it goes beyond mindless eating and becomes a tangible fact when you catch the eating activity on a notecard or in a journal. When truth looks you in the face, all your excuses that you "don't eat that much, so shouldn't be gaining weight" go out the window. You must determine what you should eat and write down what you will eat on a regular basis after you have established your poor eating habits.

Since the old habits are so deeply rooted in your mind and character, it will take staunch dedication to change on your part. Don't do the assignment alone. To support you through the transition from poor eating habits to healthy ones, find an accountability buddy.Always note that suddenly, the bad habits did not pop up, and they are not going to change that easily either. Always note that bad habits will not suddenly stop popping up; they are not going to change easily. For good and bad eating habits, build a system of incentives and punishments for yourself.

I would be the first to state that improving your eating habits is an exceedingly hard undertaking, but the obvious fact is that we live in a world where poor eating habits are rampant. It is also true that heart attacks, cancer, and many other deadly diseases are also rampant in our society. It is important that you evaluate what you eat and immediately make the decision to adjust. It could be too late next month or next year. This is for your protection.

Changing Eating Habits

There are many diets plans available on the market today. You might have tried any number of them, perhaps with varying degrees of success. You may be shocked, though, to find that you don't need a regimen to lose weight permanently; you just need to take an honest look at your current eating habits and recognize ways to improve those habits.

You would have a greater chance of permanent weight loss if you were to change only one of your eating habits than with many of the diet plans that are available today. However, the more eating habits you can change over a period of time, the more influence you'll eventually have over your weight.

If you take eating habits one at a time, changing them does not have to be that difficult. The strategy you are looking for is to concentrateon one eating pattern improvement within a set 30 day period. A new or changed habit, worked on for just 30 days, would become a permanent fixture in your mind and, thus, your daily life.

The most promising part of this technique is that you do not need to leave out all the foods that you enjoy. When we talk about changing habits, it does not mean you have to absolutely avoid certain food or drink. It could imply just a small improvement in your eating patterns, and the desired outcome will still be achieved.

It may not always be what you eat always; it may be more of an eating scenario. The fact that eating at the wrong time of day can be just as big a concern as the quantity of food you consume is one of the most amazing effects of recognizing and changing your eating habits.

It all starts with a truthful and thorough review of your daily and weekly eating habits. When the list is full, it is time to select just one habit that you want to alter when you eat or drink. You will now focus on that single habit until it is changed or entirely replaced by a new habit.

Obesity, toxicity, and infections are all tragic facts that are still faced by the human body. The way we eat food and what we eat (our food choices), however, are also the top reasons why our bodies suffer more than ever from diseases and toxicity. Our physical body bears the effects when our eating habits are not good.

Old habits die hard, as they claim. Also, with food, people generally build unconscious behaviors. We purchase the same food from the same grocery store, cook the same recipes over and over again, stop every day at the same coffee and snack shop, and live according to our own familiar routines. The eating habits we create also become automatic when it comes to our food choices. Especially now that modern life demands that we always be quick on our toes, rushing from one thing to the other, it seems that it is more convenient to eat less healthy food from fast food joints, the common option. However, over time, your health may be affected by this ease of eating just about anything in arm's reach.

Unfortunately, it also takes something drastic to causes us to pause and take a look at our lifestyle habits and eating behaviors, such as having a severe illness or becoming highly toxic. You do not need to wait too long, however! Stopping these automatic, harmful eating habits and beginning to develop new, healthier ones is the best way to break out of the unhealthy eating loop.

This is not always straightforward, because the thing about a habit is that we get so set in our ways that we convince ourselves that it's difficult to give up those old habits. Here are five quick steps to turn poor eating patterns into healthy ones:

1. Evaluate the culprit to find out. You first have to understand what's wrong with your eating habits in order to strengthen them. This is better achieved for a short period of time by keeping a food log; 3 to 5 days works well. It will give you a good idea of which areas of your eating patterns need some focus and fixing up by keeping track and writing down what you have actually consumed for a day. You may notice that, during your afternoon break, you still catch a succulent snack, or that after dinner you prefer to consume more fatty foods. You can, for example, take a slice of fruit or some raw vegetables instead of working for the afternoon by knowing where to look, or have a 1⁄2 cup of plain Greek yogurt after dinner to fulfill the emotional need for warmth by knowing exactly how you can remedy these unhealthy health behaviors. To associate your emotional relationship with food, it is also important to jot down your emotions or what you were doing while you ate.

2. Start with steps that are small. Making major, rapid, and drastic changes in eating habits can lead to changes in short-term habits and weight loss, but you won't necessarily be healthier in the long term. The priority emphasis is to be healthier on a long-term basis. Improving your eating habits permanently takes a proactive approach and does not happen overnight. You build a healthy outlook and a new partnership with food by taking baby steps towards changing your eating habits. You can start by cutting down and replacing your unhealthy food options (smaller portions, less frequently) with healthier ones (eating vegetables, waiting 5 minutes to see if you're really hungry, or going for a walk instead). When you're really hungry, it's also important to teach yourself to eat and stop when you're comfortably full. By changing your diet and eating habits little by little, you can get used to them after a while and gradually adapt them permanently to your lifestyle.

3. You'll do better if you know better. Giving greater attention to what you eat and drink is an important initial step towards conquering poor eating habits. You need to know that reading nutrition labels and keeping your food portions in mind is both beneficial and important. Your food journal can also help you to build better eating habits. When you become more conscious of what you eat, you will begin to understand how your diet needs to be changed. The cause also benefits from educating yourself on leading a more healthy lifestyle.

4. Make a deliberate effort to remove stimuli. Creating healthy eating habits means not only knowing what is wrong with your diet but also attempting to fix it and

not going back to eating the foods that cause it. You may want to find a new treat that you can indulge in, such as replacing standard ice cream with plain frozen yogurt, if sweets cause you to overeat. At the moment you feel hungry, you should start asking yourself: "can I do anything different that would be healthier?". You can also adhere to your new eating habits even when eating out or during celebrations by opting to consume foods that are nutritious or carry your own healthy snack instead.

5. Give it time and enjoy all the little accomplishments on the way. Don't expect to turn any bad eating habits into good ones overnight. Know that this is a step, and it may be a progressive one, but it depends on you. For every little accomplishment you make for yourself, don't forget to give yourself a pat on the back. Even an easy alternative to selecting a slice of wheat bread for breakfast instead of a slice of white bread is still a good start and must be celebrated!

At first it can be daunting and frustrating to eat healthily and build better eating habits, but once you see for yourself how amazing it makes you feel and how it impacts your overall wellbeing, you will discover it is worth all your efforts.

Stop Bad Eating Habits.

Is it difficult for you to avoid eating fast food even if you know what poor eating habits are doing to your abdominals, or, at the hint of some tension in your mind, you go on an eating spree?

You can see that it's all in your head. You know it, don't you? The only question is how you train your mind so that if these bad behaviors threaten your life, you will stop them.

The strategy is to make suggestions to your mind so that it embraces them, and your mind itself can help fight your binge eating disorder next time. But can a quick idea to your mind help so easily cure your poor eating habit? Yes and no is the reaction. No, since the exact system of making hypnotic suggestions must be known to you; and yes, by self-hypnosis, you can cure your binge eating. This IS feasible. We're going to tell you how.

Hypnosis works by making suggestions to the inner mind, not to the physical, waking mind. This is a difference that is essential. Every waking moment, the outer mind is busy calculating the external world and making decisions. Your self-confidence, your strengths and weaknesses, your secret talents, and shortcomings, however, are controlled by the inner mind. The inner mind, the subconscious mind, is you, the real you, and the decision-making organ is the outer mind. So, you can change yourself, your unhealthy eating habits, your binge eating disorders, and the like by just shifting your inner mind. You can eventually recover from almost any bad habit, such as smoking, procrastination, rage, etc.

We are now at the phase of how self-hypnosis works and how you can hypnotize yourself and improve your binge eating disorder to cure your unhealthy eating habits.

You begin by lying in a comfortable position and ordering your body to relax slowly. You ask step by step from your toe, then your legs and body, etc. to relax and see that your whole body is slowly loosening and in a good, relaxed state. Your mind is likewise comfortable and in a sleepy mood. Your outer mind is kind of 'sleeping,' and your inner mind is focusing. It is then that the suggestions are made to your inner mind and it will obey; you can then manage to rid yourself of any eating disorder.

For the best performance, however, the suggestions you make must be in the right format, and there are strategies by which you can make the suggestions to your mind.

Anchoring.

A bad habit is most frequently caused by a feeling of tension. You might hear the news that your mother-in-law is coming to visit you, and that may cause an anxious feeling inside you, causing you to fall unconsciously into an eating binge.

The response is: you must have a way to replace it with a nice feeling as soon as you get the upsetting trigger.

So, what you're doing is imagining a beautiful scene, like a beach or some other location you've been and want to return to. Picture yourself being there, feeling the sand under your feet, the wetness of the surf soaking your feet, the sun on your face, the wind ruffling your hair, the scent of the shore, the sight of the rising sea waves, the white surf, etc.

Then, with a few of your fingertips on your forehead, this is the essential part of repairing the picture and feeling. So, later on, if you brush your forehead with your fingertips, a fun vision wafts over you of the swelling sea. This way, at the present moment, you get over your stress and substitute it with this fun view.

Restoring Your Health Through Mindful Eating.

Have you started thinking about how to regain or sustain your healthy eating habits and overall wellbeing now that the holidays and their distractions are behind you? The holiday season can be overwhelming and cause your goals to be poorly organized. Instead of having health and wellbeing at the top of your agenda, did it slip to the bottom as you organized parties and shopped for presents?

Sometimes, with a few extra pounds of weight, you can feel sluggish, exhausted, and sometimes even depressed. Do you experience these post-holiday health blues? Keep reading to determine how to improve your health and reverse the adverse effects on you that the holiday season had.

Use food as medicine and in a conscientious way approach feeding. What is eating with mindfulness? Mindful eating is not a meal plan or diet; instead, it's an evolving wellness strategy that encourages an understanding of what's happening in your body and mind. This allows you to become conscious of your psychological and physiological reasons to eat. You are better able to align what you consume, the way you eat, and why you eat by engaging in thoughtful eating.

Tune into physical characteristics of food.

Three of the senses are involved in tuning into the physical characteristics of food: smell, taste, and sight. You take in the scent, the fragrance of the food. Keep in mind how it feels. Is it a good smell? Take note of how it tastes in your mouth with flavor and whether it satisfies your taste buds. Note in your mouth how it tastes and if you like the texture. With sight, how is it going to look? Is it attractive to you? Use your mind's eye to imagine yourself enjoying what you eat.

Tune into daily habits and the process of eating.

Note the patterns of everyday eating. Take into account what times of the day you eat and what things you do that can lead to mindless eating. These involve watching TV while you eat, eating while writing emails at your desk, or standing above the sink, shoving food into your mouth. Take note about who else is present and what they may consume when eating; often, we consume only because the other person eats or is present.

Tune into mindless eating triggers.

There are some behaviors, events, locations, emotions, and individuals that can stimulate your eating habits and cause you to binge while you are not even aware of it. Tune in to mindless eating triggers. You have to remember to become conscious of what causes you to feed. Take a close look at your physical, emotional, and environmental reasons. If you know how to identify your causes before you plunge, you can better predict them and catch yourself, and maybe even start improving your behaviors.

Mindful eating is a commitment for the long term and requires a lot of practice. Observation is the principal key to this method. First, you need to learn to observe the symptoms of your body, such as hunger, satiety, and level of energy. Second, by being mindful of your emotions and emotional stimuli, you must observe your psychological condition. You can get lots of details from studying your mind and body.

Practice staying in the moment. Most of us work on autopilot most of the time, so this is easier said than done. Often, rather than being at the moment, it's easier to fall back on habit or routine. Taking the merriment and fun out of life with habit and routine will leave you feeling cold and numb. People also eat in an attempt to fill the gap, but mindless eating will just widen it instead. You are more likely to note things when they happen if you are present in the moment. In addition, you are more conscious of how your food tastes, smells, sounds in your mouth, and whether your appetite is fulfilled or leaves you feeling full and slow. Practice being in the moment while driving, or while involved in other tasks and multitasking by avoiding eating in front of the screen.

Humans suffer from numerous disorders of the digestive tract, such as hemorrhoids. Blood vessels around the axis of our lower rectal region at the rear end are inflamed and contaminated by hemorrhoids. The last portion of the colon attached to the large intestines is the rear end. When left untreated, hemorrhoids can be very upsetting and distressing. It can impact you at home, at work, and in various aspects of your everyday life.

Hemorrhoids are rising and increasing annually to around 75 percent of individuals. People around the age of 40 to 50 will have a 65% chance of having one. The older we grow, the greater the chances of having hemorrhoids. The numerous aspects that can cause hemorrhoids should be very careful.

Hemorrhoids can be caused by many factors:

1. Chronic digestive disorders, diarrhea, or excessive ingestion of softeners or laxatives.

2. Straining can hinder the normal function of the veins in the anal region during bowel movements.

3. Sitting in the bathroom for long periods may cause the veins to become inflamed, causing pain and scratching.

4. Constipation can lead to an inflammation of the blood vessels and to a fall from their normal position.

5. The risk of hemorrhoids is also raised by a lack of fiber in the diet or bad eating habits.

When seeking to prevent hemorrhoids, it can be very effective to follow a mindful diet and implement lifestyle changes. It also helps to decrease inflammation and relieves symptoms. Simple changes in our dietary patterns and everyday activities will prevent this illness. Mindful eating will avoid worsening and unfavorable hemorrhoids. A safe bowel habit can be developed by consuming the correct food and having the right exercise. One must stop sitting down and standing up for prolonged periods of time. Strong lifting should also be avoided because it can produce unnecessary pressure on the veins.

Drinking water also helps the body a great deal. Water controls the circulation of the blood and brings nutrients through the bloodstream to cells. It also eliminates toxins and waste, which is essential.

Here are answers about how hemorrhoids can be minimized and prevented:

Foods for Hemorrhoids Prevention and Cure:

1. Fruits: fiber-rich raspberries, pears, avocados, bananas, oranges, grapefruit, and other fruits.

2. Vegetables: green peas, spinach, broccoli, squash, and other mixed vegetables.

3. Fluids: water, the juice from fruits, and juice from vegetables.

Food to be avoided:

1. Alcohol or beverages that are refined.

2. Refined sugar and white flour.

3. Processed meat.

4. Foods that are high in fat.

5. Gâteaux and cookies.

For safe living, it is always be best to ask experts for advice and support. It is significant to be aware of one's own health.

"Simplicity is the ultimate sophistication," as Da Vinci said; keeping things straightforward is more difficult than complicating things. Quick measures to strengthen your eating habits require you to make things easy and pleasant because, if you don't, you're the one with a rough time on your hands. Keep in mind that changing your eating habits will improve your lifestyle. Keeping it easy will also help you excel and will not eventually harm you.

To change your eating habits, the following are some simple steps.

Do eat your meals on a regular schedule. Skipping or pushing a meal forward can have repercussions. When you miss a meal, you tend to gorge on the next one, and sometimes pure hunger makes you consume more calories than you need. Advancing will also help you eat more at your next meal, as it will be long enough between them to help you hungry again.

Eat parts sparingly. The way to go is to keep things small and easy. It will help you improve your dietary habits if you ensure your portions are appropriate sizes. Don't have substitutes, such as an extra slice of steak, an extra serving of mashed potatoes, or an extra piece of cake; just be pleased with what you've already eaten. A smaller plate may also be used. You would have less room on your plate this way and make it appear to be packed with food.

For every meal that you consume, maintain a reasonably good balance. Eat just three meals a day, and, if you can, skip snacks. Even if we can't stop eating fast foods, even though we want to, most of us operate at a really fast rate and it is convenient, so don't feel bad, because you can make up for it. Be sure to consume less and better for the next meal, for example, at dinner if you have had a high-calorie meal for lunch. Get some salads or light foods with low calories that will compensate for what you took earlier that day.

The secret is moderation. Too much and too many is a big no-no. Too little or even not getting any is a taboo. When you think it's unhealthy, never exclude the essential food from your diet. An example is, for instance, sugar: too much is going to make you unhealthy, too little is going to slow you down, and none of this is going to make you hypoglycemic.

All items, as long as they are appropriate and moderate, are fine.

The best are natural foods. It will help you to change your eating habits if you eat as many natural products as possible. Imagine you somehow replaced your habit of eating those burgers and fries with eating tons of veggies, fruits, whole grains, healthy fats, beans, and seeds. Wouldn't that be a life worth eating for? Many people do not consume enough of these natural foods; they consume packaged meals that are useful instead. Natural foods will help you balance your hormones with the nutrients and natural chemicals on those foods and decrease cravings for other foods.

CHAPTER FOUR

POSITIVE AFFIRMATIONS

FOR WEIGHT LOSS

The only thing that is important when it comes to health and fitness is a balanced bodyweight. What decides your health is your weight! That's why, any time you go for a checkup, doctors always check your weight. The problem today is that people do not look at weight loss as a health problem anymore, instead considering it as more of a a LOOKS problem, which is why they don't get anywhere. If they could only understand how important weight is to health, people would be more inspired to lose weight.

Your weight makes you who you really are. Whether you like it or not, you will be judged by it; this is just part of life. In fact, in America alone, over 65% of the population is either overweight or obese. That's two out of every three Americans. There are over 1 billion individuals worldwide that fall into this group! That's 1 in every 7 people around the world who have weight issues! It's no wonder healthcare is such a big issue.

So, you need to lose weight quickly and lose it right away, whether you're overweight or obese, but how are you going to lose weight the best way? The response to that is the biggest hidden weight loss mystery. The basic fact is that individuals DON'T know how to lose weight. In hopes that it will succeed, many will only try the old eat less and exercise more theory. Nonetheless, this mentality of weight loss is what ultimately keeps the world the same way with the same issues. People only do whatever the media and so-called experts tell them while doing the little operation. This is because there is no balance, which is why many struggle to lose weight!

The key to weight loss is balance. Every day, you need to eat the correct number of calories and exercise for the correct amount of time each week. For overall and long-term results, getting the balance is the best way! It's so important to understand because the secret of equilibrium can go to such endless depths.

However, you need to be well informed about it and its relationship with weight loss to make use of balance. You need to learn more about weight loss and all the elements of it. If you're serious about weight loss, then you can spend some of your time learning the secrets of weight loss. It's not going to be that hard if you know what there is to know about it.

If you want to really go further into weight loss, you're going to find there's so much more to it. Many factors have to be considered, including a good diet, weight, metabolism, and even the human body itself! In order to grasp weight loss entirely, there are so many things to remember.

You must first become educated about weight loss if you really want to commit to it. You need to get to the point where you will be able to spot it immediately if you make a mistake, without any support from experts or professionals. To succeed, you need to be totally alone.

The Question.

Imagine scaling the mountain to ask the wise man what the secret is to losing weight? As is always the case with the wise person on the mountain top, their answer is not only short and simple, but also obvious and common sense.

The Reaction.

So, in response to the issue of the key to weight loss, the wise individual advises, first of all, to not gain weight.

Follow-Up Question and Reaction.

I asked the follow-up question to this one: If I knew how, O wise man, I would not have climbed the mountain.

The wise individual answers: In the first place, the way to reach weight loss is not to gain weight. Find the four keys to losing weight in order not to gain weight in the first place.

The Four Secrets.

O wise man, what are the four secrets to losing weight? Again, I ask, but the wise person is somehow gone. When I walk down the mountain, all I can think about is what the secrets are. The path down is long, giving time for the individual to think about the conversation. Then it dawns on me that the answer has to be brief, concise, clear, common sense. The four weight loss secrets must be:

Eat Less - Eat Right - Enjoy Activity - Enjoy Life.

Hey, how real. The wise person has enabled me to find the final weight loss ties and to know that there are no magic bullets, but rather that it is the balancing act of eating and living and enjoying life.

Eat Less.

The first of the four secrets to losing weight is eating less. More easily said than done, you may say. I accept that. Portion control is the largest problem. Over the years, the portions have expanded not only in our homes but also in our restaurants and also in our plate size. What was considered to be a normal daily portion several years ago is considered a junior portion now! Then again, who could avoid an offer and pick the bigger size, which is always only a little more pricey and enticing?

Eating less, however, is truly the first step. Just dish out a bit less. Don't go for second helpings. Do not super-size your meal. Stop clearing your plate. Send the doggy bag along. If it's hard at first, try and try again. Try a natural appetite suppressant called hoodia, if anything else fails. Be selective about your brand choice, however. There are several labels that are not pure and packed with fillers. Make sure that it is grown by an independent laboratory in South Africa and certified pure.

Eat Right.

The second of the four secrets is Eating Right. Eating right is about not just what you eat and drink, but what you eat and how you eat — it is necessary to chew enough and eat slowly. A big issue for the overweight is eating wrong. It is worth exploring the use of a diet plan that helps you pursue a consistent approach to eating correctly.

There are numerous services on the market available and sold in hospitals, varying from low to very high rates. Nonetheless, do not fall for the ads that announce a single strategy as the best. The best program is the program that suits your personality and adapts to your lifestyle; the program which is most suitable for you. This implies that you need to identify the different choices to decide the best match for you. No short cuts and quick answers are available — no one would be overweight if it were.

Enjoy Activity.

Humans need activity. The third secret is to be occupied: play sports, walk, take the steps rather than the elevator, keep the car on the driveway and instead walk over. It is also about taking up a hobby that will get you out and about. Many of these tasks, because we are social creatures, include engaging with others, which is also a positive thing.

Enjoy Life.

Life is perhaps the most important of the four secrets; it's all about enjoying the simple things that don't necessarily take a great deal of money, energy, or time. This can be achieved by anyone; it is not just for the well off. Get a good outlook and look for the brighter side. Enjoy yourself, your family, and your friends. Enjoy what you do at work and what you do at home. Indulge yourself in hobbies. Learn new things and have an inquisitive mind, asking questions and obtaining replies. They all contribute to a loving life.

The dictionary definition of affirmationis the affirmation of which is already known. Affirmations of health are valuable tools for encouraging one's self to reach an optimal state of being. If you want to lose any kilos, weight loss claims might be very beneficial for you. If you really want to slash those extra pounds, it is the very first thing you should be doing.

Affirmations of weight loss might consist of emphasizing and agreeing to yourself that you just have to reinforce with yourself that you have to do away with it because you want to increase your weight when you are about to get tempted to eat. It is something that will direct you not to slip back into your old habits, but will instead help you move on to accomplish that objective instead.

It might be a slogan, a mantra, or whatever else you'd like to call it. In order to reduce your urge, the trick here is to send constructive messages to your brain. There is more possibility for you to slim down through this. It's supposed to be something you trust and something that will keep you on track.

When you mention them in the present tense, the affirmations will be far clearer. Do not use the future tense as this just puts off what you want to do now. It will give you a much deeper belief that you are ready and that you want to do this now if you place your affirmations in the present tense. Right now, it's going to happen, and it's not something you're going to have to do in the future.

Your attitude and how you use your vocabulary play a very important role in your comments. According to Barbara Hoberman Levine, author of "Your Body Believes in Every Word You Say", if you want to concentrate on not doing it, the more your mind and body align to make a deliberate effort to do it.

People who want to lose weight will find a fight every day against cravings and temptations.

Here is where the allegations come in. As a personal motto, the very individual should "own" the affirmations, not borrow from anyone else. You will suggest phrases such as "I'm on the fitness track" or "I love how I feel today".

Write it out and place them in a location that is part of your everyday routine — say, your bathroom mirror — to make your affirmations even stronger. Before going to bed, read them to yourself each morning and every night.

Some psychologists also recommend that you snap your fingers and count how many snaps you made that day every time you come across a negative post. Analyze this and come up with a better, more practical affirmation.

Weight loss affirmations are just a mental roadmap for you to meet your target weight. In this pursuit, your mind and your body should be one.

One way you can condition your mind for the success of weight loss is by using positive affirmations.

What are positive affirmations?

Positive words are strong words that we repeat (either in our mind or out loud) to ourselves, and they are usually things we want to do. They are used to stimulate our inner thoughts and to affect our behavior and the progress we make. If you say them frequently with confidence and true conviction, then your subconscious mind will come to recognize them as genuine. Your new positive self-image will be improved, and you will be charged with positive energy. Your mindset, actions, and thoughts will shift and bring about a positive change until your mind begins to believe something is real. Positive remarks can be customized to any purpose you want to reach, including losing weight.

Weight Loss Positive Affirmations.

You need to use a handful of motivating weight loss phrases that will inspire you and reflect what you want to accomplish.

Here are some ideas for helpful weight loss statements:

- For me, losing weight comes easily.
- I will attain my targets for weight loss.
- Every day I lose weight.
- I love the taste of nutritious food.
- I have power over how much I eat.
- I do enjoy exercising; it makes me do feel healthy.
- I am getting fitter and stronger through exercise.
- I am cultivating more balanced eating habits all the time.
- Every day I get slimmer.
- I look and feel amazing.

Try to use optimistic phrases that work for you and that you feel comfortable with. You have to repeat them regularly (at least 3-4 times a day) and with real certainty in order for them to work. Repeat them when you wake up in the morning and the last thing before you go to bed. Saying them out loud can be very motivational if you can get time alone. Write down your optimistic affirmations on a card and bring them around with you for an immediate boost at any time. You might also be able to post them on your fridge, a brilliant way to make you think twice about unhealthy snacks.

How's your loss of weight going? Are you losing the weight you thought you were going to lose? The expectations we set for losing weight often do not necessarily align with the actual act of losing weight. It can be really tempting to feel like it's pointless at times such as this, to just forget it and give up, then go back to the old way of eating.

In addition to keeping you on track with your weight loss goals, optimistic words can be incredibly helpful by inspiring you to stay on this healthy track every day.

Affirmations and visualizations are tools that are used to accomplish almost anything in life, and there is no exception when it comes to weight loss. If that is so, why do so many people insist that statements don't work?

They need to be carried out properly in order for them to work. Some individuals feel that they can master a specific subject simply by seeking knowledge here and there. Quite often, in order to achieve success, a mastery of the subject is necessary.

The mediocre life that individuals build for themselves because of their negative thinking is a clear example of statements at work. Poor thinking plays a part in daily comments.

When you think negatively when you keep repeating, "I'm overweight, I hate the way I look, I'm never going to lose weight, it just doesn't work" etc. This is like a catch-22. The best way to have control of your life is to turn your detrimental affirmations into constructive ones.

Note, it's not easy to do. Negative thinking is a custom, and it takes a deliberate, persistent effort to break a habit.

How to Use Affirmations and Visualizations For Successful Weight Loss.

Rule 1: never use phrases that are negative. Affirmations are directed towards the subconscious mind, and negative phrases are not defined by the subconscious mind. For instance, if you say "I am no longer overweight", the subconscious mind focuses on the "overweight" aspect and ensures that you stay overweight because it sees it as something you want.

Rule 2: using the claims only in the present tense. Do not say, "With this program, I will lose weight"; instead say, "I weigh 120 pounds right now" (if your target weight is 120 pounds).

Rule 3: be insistent. Don't give up ever. Everything you have now in your life is because of years of poor thinking. It will take some time before you begin to see good things about your life, but often you will be shocked by how easily things can change.

What keeps you from reaching your weight loss target? There may be several causes and explanations, such as medicine or disease, to blame for difficulty losing unnecessary pounds.

A hormonal imbalance can interfere with weight gain fluctuations. Emotional tension and adverse thoughts can dampen your spirits and send conflicting messages to your body. Just like your goals, a negative body image and attitude may also cause your body to respond.

Using helpful weight loss tips and motivation will set you on a healthy path, while melting fat cells to balance your body and mind.

10 Simple Weight Loss Tips and Motivation.

May these simple steps help to improve you, but bear in mind that you are the one who can help you the most.

1. Picture your goals. Build imaginary images of you in your head at your target weight. Imagine that you eat healthily every day, workout with energy, and watch your weight drop on the scale. Create a vision board for nutritious eating, exercise, clothing that you want to blend in, flexing muscles, etc. In order to step towards the images you have produced in your head, visualization will positively impact your brain and emotions.

2. Celebrate victories. When you eat a healthy snack, pat yourself on the back; do the same when you work out daily, snub candy, etc. Any victory is worth the celebration, no matter how small. When it comes to a favorite activity, enjoy it. Don't use food as a reward.

3. Small steps always constitute steps. Every step that you take is still a step towards your goal. It's not necessary for you to take huge leaps. Congratulate yourself for going forward.

4. Keep positive. Your body will respond to what is being said by your mind. Put a stop to poor self-degradation habits. Start new constructive thought habits.

5. Drink a lot of water. Water has so many advantages, including improving your mood and giving you energy.

6. Self-assertions. Every day, remind yourself that you deserve it and are worth it.

7. Stay away from pessimistic individuals. Keep away from people who do not help you or who are negative. Spend time with other individuals who are inspired.

8. Don't think about uncertainty. Setbacks arise if you attempt to make progress. Don't mull them over. Just get back up, keep walking, and keep moving forward.

9. Be grateful for your body. It is a miracle and possesses untapped potential. Be thankful for this amazing gift. If you are thankful for it on a daily basis, your body will respond in a positive way and stop fat cell growth.

10. Write down your objectives. Acknowledge and pin-up your goals in a visual location. Be specific about what objectives you're aiming to achieve.

Proper Mindset for Weight Loss.

It often eludes us that our mind is responsible for our performance, or lack of it, in achieving goals that we set out to achieve in life, and this involves weight loss. Everything we want to accomplish in life begins with the power of thought; with that being said, we should understand that the kinds of thoughts we think are important. By focusing on the following three tips to help shift your mindset to a positive mode, you'll be well on a great path to achieving your weight loss goals.

Surround yourself with positive thoughts and people.

To be clear, a positive mindset is essential to moving ahead and accomplishing your weight loss goals. Use positive affirmations or creative visualization, for example, to help you change your mindset to focus on the positive. You have to be very mindful of who you surround yourself with, as this might affect your energy and how you think.

In addition, love yourself and be very gentle with yourself! You are a human being, so if you're having a troubled day or happen to be a bit off track with your weight loss goals, it's OK. Love yourself, accept your self-being, and get back on track with a hug and gentle nudge.

Be clear and precise on why you want to lose weight.

It's essential that you're very clear as to your reason for losing weight. If you're losing it for someone else, then you're doing it for the wrong reasons. You're the most significant person in your life, and in order to focus on you and your goals, it's essential you realize this. Plus, when you're doing it for someone else, you're placing yourself in a position of possible disappointment simply because of how the other individual will respond; if it's not positive or how you expected, it can put a damper on your overall success.

Set reasonable goals.

If you set yourself up for failure by setting unrealistic goals for yourself, then you're definitely making weight loss a lot harder than it has to be for you. When we don't meet our goals, it often puts us in a negative mode of thinking and visualization, leading to us beating ourselves up, so set realistic and reachable goals, and be sure to reward yourself every time you attain your goal! AND, if you do happen to miss the goal, again, be gentle to yourself, love yourself, and simply push yourself to get back on track to continue to strive to meet your goals (because at some point, you will!).

Life is supposed to be joyful, even when you're on a weight loss plan! These tips are sure to help you shift your mindset to a positive mode of thinking that will help you to accomplish all of your life goals, including weight loss. By maintaining a positive mindset, you'll be able to maintain your new health, happiness, and body much easier, too!

Creating a Vision Board to Lose Weight

To some, daydreaming may seem like a lazy way to pass the time, but in actuality, daydreaming can actually help you shape your future and allow you to realize your full potential. As far as weight loss is concerned, many of us are unhappy with the way we look and may possess a negative body image. Daydreaming or visualizing about having the ideal body can actually provide the motivation you need to create a slimmer you. One important visualization tool that can provide you with inspiration in your quest for weight loss is a vision board.

What is a Vision Board?

A vision board is a path to visually stimulate your mind into achieving the goals that you set for yourself. There are no wrong or right paths to make a vision board: it is simply what will work best for you. You can use a cork board, poster board, or even your computer to create a collage of visual images that will provide you with inspiration and motivation to attain your ideal body image.

How Does It Work?

Essentially, the vision board is said to trigger the universal Law of Attraction. The Law of Attraction primarily says that we will bring or attract into our lives the things which we focus the most attention on. Based on this law, if we are focusing on the negative, we may attract negative aspects to our life. The vision board is therefore a highly effective visualization tool since it helps us stay focused on the positive aspects of our goals. This is why many people use vision boards as motivation for weight loss.

Creating Your Ideal Body Image.

Do you have photographs of yourself that you absolutely love? Pictures from a time when you were at your ideal weight? How do those photographs make you feel? If they stimulate a positive feeling, you should definitely put them on your vision board. You should always use photographs, quotes, poetry, and affirmations that evoke a powerful and positive feeling. This will help you learn to achieve a good body image and help you see yourself in a more positive light. Using the philosophy of the Law of Attraction, your vision board will allow you to draw the things you desire into your life. A positive body image, motivation for weight loss, and eating foods that are healthy are all within your reach.

Staying on Track.

Be sure to place your vision board where it will be the most effective. It should be in a place where you will see it every day: on the refrigerator, over your desk, or in your bedroom are some examples of strategic places where the board will prove to be most valuable. As you begin to reach your weight loss goals and your body begins to change, be sure to update your board to keep your motivation going.

Learning Affirmations is an Essential Step to a Slimmer You.

It could be said that there are literally dozens of proven and effective ways of programming your subconscious mind for weight loss hypnosis. However, out of all the hypnosis for weight loss techniques, none have the lasting power and motivating effect of positive affirmations. Why? Because it's a basic skill for lifelong success as your new slimmer self, well worth the time it takes to learn the skill, including how to write and use your affirmations, how to integrate them into your daily routine, and how to add them to your regular exercise. This article will explain how to use affirmations with hypnosis for weight loss.

Many people never even try to use weight loss affirmations with hypnosis because they think it's just too hard. The funny thing about affirmations in hypnosis is that they are in fact easy and fast to learn. This is the little secret strategy you're about to learn. Now that I have your focus and you are reading my thoughts, you will very soon find yourself in the same place.

It can take months for some clients to fully learn hypnosis for weight loss. I spent four weeks with Colin "under my wing". He studied some of the most effective personal enhancement techniques, and he studied almost all the tight-lipped secrets that weight loss hypnosis has to offer. However, once he began using three basic sentences, each day in three different settings, that was when he realized the improvements had taken place.

A basic formula for using affirmations and weight loss hypnosis is available. On an index card, you write down each and every one of your optimistic affirmations. Each day, you can take out a new card and re-affirm your statement. You can only start up again when you get to the end of the cards. You could have as few as three cards, or one for every day of the year. It comes down to whatever works for you best. The following are some examples of affirmations.

When it comes to affirmations, everyone is special, but here are the top three that I found with Colin. When you practice hypnosis for weight loss, you will find that you have your own favorites. "Day by day, I am getting slimmer and slimmer in every way." This is an old affirmation that has been around for years and has a compounding impact on the subconscious mind when properly repeated. "I am happy, safe, prosperous, and smart" and "I now have everything I need for permanent weight loss". Use these three affirmations as a start, and you can build ones that work for you with practice. Use them as follows.

In different settings, you may want to use these optimistic affirmations at least three times per day, includingwhen you work out and before you go to sleep at night. You could even incorporate them into your morning walk to work. One instance is to say something when you work out, like "I have a fantastic body" and "I love my body". You are programming yourself with optimistic thinking, good emotions, and new habits that will affect you, even though you don't believe that this is valid. These new affirmations will soon become your normal way of thinking, and repeating them over and over again will create a condition of self-fulfillment for you. You set yourself up to win.

"As I balance my lifestyle, my body continues to improve", "I love the food that makes me slim", "weight loss is effortless", and "I enjoy being well" are all great examples. Many classes teaching weight loss hypnosis have motivated individuals to use these affirmations. They have a long track record and are known to function within a period as short as 21 days. It is also beneficial to document yourself reading out your affirmations with strength and enthusiasm. Before you go to bed and when you wake in the morning, read your index cards. As you go to work, tell yourself: "With each and every breath I take, I get slimmer and slimmer and slimmer with each and every step." Isn't the work of affirmations and weight loss hypnosis more than worth it?

In order to make your change last, it will take some engagement and constant effort on your part. So, make sure to learn and use these sample affirmations and produce your own weight loss script hypnosis. Do the exercises, and compose and add your own affirmations that relate to you into your everyday life. The drug has been prescribed to you, and now it's your turn to take it.

CHAPTER FIVE

DAILY WEIGHT LOSS MOTIVATION

WITH MINI HABITS

Having a weight loss regimen to stick to is not enough for you. So as to help yourself thrive and meet your weight goals, there are many aspects you need to integrate into your regimen on a regular basis. There will be days when you note that you really can't seem to meet your weekly / monthly goals, no matter your determination to try to stick to your weight loss program. Because of this, you tend to lack motivation for everyday weight loss, slack on your schedule, and, finally, give up altogether. OK, here are some things you can start doing on a regular basis to help you succeed in losing weight on your journey.

Sleep Right, Start Right.

If you didn't get a decent night's sleep, your day wouldn't start right, so be sure to have regular hours of sleep. On average, you can have up to 7-8 hours of sleep a night, and nothing less than 4 hours. If you are among those people with insomnia or other sleeping problems, ask your doctor for advice on relieving your symptoms.

Eat Right, Start Right.

Before beginning your day, eat a good breakfast. Energize yourself with a good serving of vegetables, whole grain, oats, juice, or tea. Take in nutritious foods that will simultaneously fill you up and reduce your cholesterol. Studies have shown that, while hunger increases appetite, people who deprive themselves by missing breakfast eat more during the day.

Start right, Drink Right.

Keep hydrated and drink a minimum of 8 8 oz glasses of water every day. Water normalizes the digestive system and assists you with both detoxification and removal. Water also encourages the body to properly absorb nutrients and minerals, which in turn helps the body to become stronger and healthier, allowing you to complete the weight loss program more effectively.

Shake It, Move It.

Exercise is an important practice in your daily life and is one of the biggest obstacles to a person's motivation for daily weight loss. Some people may not find regular workouts as fun or appealing as regular trips to the mall would be. The trick to solving this is to vary your workouts and do something every day that is physically active. Instead of undertaking your regular commute by car or public transport, start walking. Dance a little, join your colleagues or community in a sporting game, undertake more strenuous house chores. Just don't stop moving, otherwise a sendentary lifestyle will definitely obstruct your progress.

Plan It, Write It.

Composing a to-do-list should become a routine. This enables you to become more efficient and effective. Write down what you want to do for today, or write down what things you want to do to reach your goals for the day that follows. Take regular time out of your day to reflect. There don't need to be any long paragraphs; there may be just fragments or sentences. What did you do correctly? In order to better yourself, what do you intend to do?

If you start right, move it, and schedule it, your inspiration for regular weight loss will certainly be increased. You will have more motivation and inspiration to stick with your weight loss programs and get to where you want to be in your life!

You will need to find ways to remain motivated every day while you are faced with the constant task of trying to lose weight. Your realistic goals, your ability to imagine what you want to do, and the degree of progress you have at the beginning are the variables that will sustain your high motivation for weight loss.

A special, concerted effort is needed for daily motivation, and it isn't always easy. Finding an Internet support network to check in with every day is one perfect way to keep the inspiration for weight loss high. On the Internet, there are several such chat groups and forums.

Another idea is to keep your growth, challenges, and achievements in a daily journal. You can keep a book of your daily diet, or write about the process and difficulty of losing weight and the feelings related to it in your journal.

The incentive for weight loss will remain fresh with something concrete that you can look at to remind you of your objectives. For instance, you can tape a picture of yourself at an ideal weight onto your refrigerator door. You can similarly buy an outfit in your perfect size and hang it in your wardrobe where you can see it every day.

The desire to lose weight cannot come from the same position every day. If you can build some strategies for keeping your everyday motivation up then you are much more likely to be successful and bounce back quickly if you have any setbacks. You don't have to face the challenge alone, regardless of what you ultimately see as your inspiration for weight loss.

Are you looking for a new thing to do that has proven results?

We appear to unconsciously do what the people that surround us are doing. Behind the scenes, our subconscious mind guides and motivates these unconscious decisions. The fear of pain and the desire for happiness drives us. It's that easy, actually.

We need to face it: we're distracted. When our plate is already full, how do we add one more activity? Below, I walk through the steps of what I call my inspiration for the morning. It takes just a couple of minutes. The trick is to substitute everything, not to add one more item to your plate. Where are you squandering time? Take a few moments to study your day to see where you are wasting time on non-productive tasks to substitute it with your inspiration for the morning!

Here are three easy steps to build your own inspiration for daily weight loss!

1. What's the 'why' for losing weight? Take a moment to imagine the true explanation for your motivation. It could be to be in a bikini on the beach, to be free of diabetes, or to ride on a roller coaster with your child. Whatever the excuse, take a moment to close your eyes and bring them to the present moment. Build the overwhelming urge to feel good that will remind you why you are going to decide to make those choices today.

2. Now, imagine your ideal day. What do you want to eat for breakfast, lunch, and dinner? Visualize what you're going to say no to and why you're motivated to choose this. Go through your day and imagine the tasks that you are going to execute for the day.

3. Finally, take a minute to experience the triumph! When you have effectively integrated your goals and are full of energy, how would you ultimately feel because you have selected nutritious food options?

It is necessary to remember that the subconscious operates with photos. Just talking about about the steps above is not the same; the steps need to be achieved by visualization. You have to see through your mind first, and then it will manifest itself into reality. If you want to integrate these three easy steps into your morning routine, I guarantee that you will be inspired to increase weight loss and start to be more consistent with your healthy lifestyle changes!

Get Rid of Obesity

Some obese patients are often desperate to easily lose fat, and it is for this reason that most of them pursue different ways to lose weight quickly. You should, however, have to compromise between having a lean and balanced body and being willing to sustain your exercise for weight loss. In addition, healthy ways of losing weight should be found so that there is no danger to life.

While there are several choices for weight loss today, obese patients should look for the right plan for weight loss. They can opt for surgery to lose weight, the effects of which can be seen in a few minutes. They can also choose how to lose weight naturally, such as getting a healthy diet and exercise. With this many ways to rapidly burn fats, being inspired is the most important thing. This is why this book would concentrate on the inspiration for weight loss to lose weight quickly.

What are these obesity weight loss motivations?

1. There's a successful performance at hand!

Progress is still at hand with the different methods of losing fats quickly. The only thing is that your balanced lifestyle needs to be upheld. You need to exercise for 15 to 20 minutes every day. You will need to maintain your diet for weight loss in order to gain control of your food. Do not be discouraged by how slow the effects of weight loss can be; it's normal that they are. Only think that it's an accomplishment every time you reach a new achievement.

2. Reduce weight by dieting correctly.

I know for a fact that it's difficult to regulate one's diet, particularly when what you're doing is already at home. This does not entirely mean that you have to crash diet; this won't help you lose weight quickly and is instead just going to make you eat and crave more food. Eating is the only thing that you can do, yet eating habits have to be monitored. You should never skip meals. You should include nutritious food in your meals that provide less fat for your body.

3. Losing weight? Why?

You need to have a justification why you're doing this to be more inspired to lose weight quickly. The explanation could be to obtain a healthier body or to prevent any sickness or disease due to obesity. Throughout the time you follow your weight loss program, your reasons for doing so will help you to stay inspired.

4. Focus on the advantages!

You will be offered incentives for weight loss by concentrating more on the benefits. Do not think that what you are doing is burdensome or boring. Focus on the effects of the exercise for weight loss, so that the mind can be focused on the long-term benefits in particular.

5. Groups for Help

In your campaign to lose weight, support groups are really helpful. Why? They will help you become empowered and feel fulfilled in what you are doing. Look for a friend or a group that has the same aims as you do. In this way, when anyone sees you doing your own thing to lose weight, you won't feel bored or threatened.

Techniques and Instances of Motivating Weight Loss

What's the secret to motivation for weight loss? Where it originate from, and why does it, for no apparent reason, seemingly vanish in a flash?

At some point, most of us embarking on this journey to better our health and fitness have encountered a jolt of inspiration, a fire that has been ignited underneath our butts, which propels us from the couch and into the gym / back-yard / park / whatever. With great appreciation, I look at those times, because without them, there is every possibility that nothing would have changed.

I wish to tell you how to get the ball rolling if you still have to make a move for yourself, but I can't. Each and every person will have a different moment of 'propulsion' depending on your lifestyle and circumstances, and your motivator will be something different. Images, a friend's statement, being faced with a seemingly simple physical challenge that suddenly becomes difficult: everyone has a different anecdote about what it was that first inspired them to stop being so unfit and change their life.

The sad fact is that motivation can easily vanish as soon as it appears. Most of us have probably witnessed this sudden vanishing act, and, quite disheartened, have turned to Google or books, looking desperately for the "magic bullet" that will hold you away from the biscuit tin, for list of ways to remain motivated, or techniques to improve motivation. Michelle Bridges, probably the most popular personal trainer in Australia, says that this magic bullet doesn't exist. She's really honest in an article in Mamamia about the fact that she doesn't especially like exercise. She does not wake up every morning feeling pumped up to go for a run or lift weights. The passion for fist-pumping is reserved for the cameras, it seems. She says, "Just do it" and avoid looking for inspiration. Exercise and making healthy food decisions must be so ingrained in your lifestyle that it becomes as natural as brushing your teeth or taking a shower. Don't worry, just do it.

To a large extent, I agree with Michelle, but I maintain that when you force yourself to get over the pain barrier, you can and will enjoy exercise. Endorphins from exercise are strong. During those times in my life that would otherwise have exhausted me, endorphins held me away from anti-depressants.

My tips for weight loss motivation.

Although I agree with Michelle's philosophy about the need to integrate exercise as naturally as possible into your daily routine, some strategies that you might turn to for inspiration on days when that's not enough include:

1. Telling yourself how you'll feel when the job is done in an hour. You will never regret exercising, but you will almost certainly regret not doing so.

2. Using pictures. Before and after pictures of other individuals who have had tremendous success, or a photo of someone doing things that you would like to be able to do, like rock climbing or a chin-up or chasing their kid around a park, maybe of yourself in the 'bad old days': keep some handy, whatever's working. Vision boards are strong stuff, even though the premise can sound a little trite.

3. Identifying yourself in the third person. I do this sometimes: "Gen is strong and fit. She lifts things and throws stuff and hikes through the mud for miles. She can run and jump and skip." Then I remind myself again that even though I did one of those things just once, I still did it, so it is already real. Live as if your dream is already real, and your purpose has already been achieved.

4. Using motivational sayings, which will work for certain individuals. Although chocolate cake can taste great, it's priceless to walk down the street and feel my flat, toned stomach under my top. I put my hand on my waist sometimes, just to marvel again at the fact that I had a waist when it was merely an illusion for so long. These things are immeasurable in order to feel light, powerful, fit, strong, and confident.

5. Taking measurements daily. I mostly suggest the waist and hips to women; of course, you can also do the upper arm, the stomach, and the leg, but you're probably going to put on your muscles here and you don't want to be discouraged. You can still weigh yourself, of course, but the scales fluctuate too much and it's natural to put on muscle weight, too. You don't want to give yourself more excuses to feel frustrated again. Measurements can be solid. I've had weeks that feels like a futile cause, and I think I'm never going to get to where I want to be, only to get the tape measure out and see that I've lost a centimeter off my waist, for instance, while feeling like I've made no progress. Know that the key is progression, not perfection.

6. Revisiting your goals if the motivation disappears for days or weeks at a time. Look at them closely and make a hard-nosed judgment about whether they are SMART: Specific, Observable, Feasible, Reasonable, and Timely. If you said, "In a year, I want to have a hot body", is that a smart goal? No, of course it's not. Anyway, what is a "hot body"? Why a year? How are you going to know when you're there? The tragic reality is that those of us who know what it's like to be overweight and unhealthy may have a self-perception that is permanently distorted and will never really believe we're "there". Instead, you might say to yourself, "I want to be able

to do ten real push-ups in 3 months" (actually on your toes, not your knees, and chest as close to the ground as you can handle). Then, the next target would be to do five one-handed push-ups within 12 months. Of course, these are just examples, chosen because of my own personal fascination with humble push-ups!

If everything else in the book fails, if you've tried every single motivational technique and yet don't feel any more motivated, it's time for a break. Don't sit for a week on your ass eating cookies, like I've been known to do, but take a good few days of mostly healthy food, as much incidental exercise as you can fit in. Read all your favorite books, and just relax. Know that you have not become overweight and unhealthy overnight, and if you give yourself a few days' breaks, you will not then stack weight back on. There's every chance you're physically and mentally drained, and for the time being, the relentless worrying and obsessing over your priorities have become too much. I know how that feels, and have witnessed it several times! Try to trust yourself and your body that the seed of good habits has been well and truly planted, and that a few days' breaks will be enough for that elusive inspiration to begin to return. There's every chance you'll skip exercise, and I find that I start to crave salad again after a few days of eating the way I used to in the old days, with big servings of carb-heavy food.

Long-term objectives are as important when it comes to weight loss as they are to everything else in life. You can then start following the required steps to make your dream a reality if you have a clear and good picture of where you are going and what you want to accomplish. A particular target is a dream with a date on it, and during your weight loss adventure, it can be a good source of inspiration. However, the target can also seem a million miles away when you have a very bad day; this is where short-term goals may help. Losing 20 pounds in a year may seem too much to do after a rough week, but you may feel much more optimistic about losing 2 pounds in a month.

If you continue to lose weight, setting short-term targets is a great way to remain motivated and concentrated. Your short-term objectives should be equal to your ultimate target, stretching you but being realistic at the same time. Break down your long-term target into smaller bits, find out what you have to do on a daily and weekly basis, and how many pounds you need to lose.

Short-term targets for weight loss will give you the chance to experience some early results and give a real boost to your self-esteem. Don't focus on the main prize, but think instead about what you need to do on a regular and weekly basis. Every mini-goal you hit will spur you on and help create some real momentum. Think hard about the healthy changes to your everyday eating habits and general lifestyle that you need to make.

For example, suggesting that you are going to eat more nutritious food is a bad target. Your expectations must not be ambiguous. However, it is a reasonable goal to suggest that you are not going to eat fries for a week and will eat at least two pieces of fresh fruit a day. You've got to make concrete and observable objectives. Vowing to do more exercise this week is a poor target, but it is much easier to aim to exercise for at least thirty minutes on four separate days in the week ahead.

Try to set at least one new target a week and fully devote all your efforts to achieving it. You should then stick doing it until you have achieved your weekly target, and until it becomes a routine and a permanent part of your lifestyle. You are then free to follow another target; you will finally end up with a lot of healthy eating and lifestyle behaviors that will result in permanent weight loss.

Here are a few suggestions for some short-term targets to make your goals as diverse as you can:

- Eat a good and nutritious breakfast on a regular basis.
- Drink eight glasses per day of water.
- Eat five fruit and vegetable portions a day.
- Cut your consumption of calories by five hundred calories a day.
- Undertake thirty minutes a day of physical activity.
- Walk to work for a week.
- Use the stairs all the time.
- Introduce a new fruit or vegetable every day for a week.
- Cut your portion sizes and use a smaller pan.

Go and make those short-term targets, stick to them, and it will take care of your long-term dream of weight loss.

You Must Be Consistent for Good Weight Loss.

Many people fail to understand that at least 10% of the total calorie intake of the human body is used in the digestive process. With this thought clearly in mind, because the body's metabolism is going high at this stage, it would seem that eating regularly would be an imposing way of holding extra weight off. Many of the best nutritionists in the nation strongly recommend that you consume at least 6 small meals a day rather than 3 larger meals.

The issue with this definition is that the amount of medical research spent on this theory is limited, and not enough studies have actually been carried out to be definitive yet. Dietitians say that if you eat 6 small meals a day and your calorie target is a mere 1,100 calories a day, then these small mini-meals won't do the trick. If you linger in a hungry state, you are tempted to snack more often, eventually defeating your weight loss program's entire intent.

Therefore, when it comes to food, the trick is to standardize your habits. How many hours a day you eat is not entirely necessary, but the main point is to do so in a consistent way. The feeding activities of each day should replicate the previous days.

One research showed that women who tended to eat the same total amount of daily meals generally consumed fewer calories than those who never had a routine. Furthermore, those women who ate randomly failed to allow their metabolism to kick in properly and reduce their excess weight, resulting in less loss of weight than the regulated community. It helps to make it easier for you to maintain a regular routine by eating meals that aim to make you feel full for a longer period of time.

The benefits of fiber in your diet may already be familiar to you, but slow-burning protein foods work just as well. It was discovered at the Washington School of Medicine that people who ate large quantities of high protein foods appeared to stave off their hunger pangs while eating fewer calories a day. By utilizing foods that are low in calories, you can effectively curb the urges to consume; this could be yogurt or fresh fruit, for example, or maybe a hard-boiled egg or some whole-grain toast. When you are trying to reach weight loss targets, don't ignore the appeal of protein-rich peanut butter spread on fresh celery sticks.

We have an abundance of comfort food in America that caters to our every wish. We have a great variety of snack chips or soups that are appropriately packed in different containers that fit conveniently into or sit next to our seat in our automotive cup holders. What our next tip really talks about is unhealthy habits when you try to find tips for your weight loss. The only thing we ought to do when we eat is eat: do not drive to and from work, do not watch TV, do nothing but eat. You expose yourself to the issues associated with "habits" by violating this golden rule. With just the food and the food alone, we want to connect with our food. I really cannot emphasize the point enough that when we are feeding, nothing else should be done.

In a study conducted many years ago, it was found that women who listened to an audiobook on tape while consuming their lunch normally consumed at least 50 more calories than those who simply ate and then returned to work. Another similar research in Finland found that only about 20% of test subjects ate because they were genuinely hungry, while the rest simply wanted to find something to do while they read a book or watched TV.

CONCLUSION

Well, the misplaced emphasis is the reason so many individuals struggle at weight loss. It's so easy. Don't ask how it works or why; it just does. Make sure to read on, or you could skip the correct use of the only major tool at your disposal: your mind.

Why is your mind's proper use important? Excessive use can potentially cause weight gain instead of weight loss. In order to get the benefits from any action you take, you need to know what happens when you concentrate on it.

Now, when I say that the main reason people struggle to lose or maintain weight is misplaced emphasis, I mean that the emphasis is placed on the exact opposite of what they should focus on.

The Law of Attraction is called the Law of the Mind. Now, before you turn away because all this sounds new-age-y, just let me tell you, it's not. It is not a modern age, nor is it anything that belongs only to some single community of individuals, religion, or whatever. The Law of Attraction is a little ambiguous, and it seems to be even more so for students, since most of them don't really know how it worksbut just want to cash in on it.

The Law of Attraction states that certain thoughts are attracted by ideas, behavior, and substance. So, when you concentrate on "losing weight", you need to lose weight more. Your body and subconscious will react accordingly to create more "weight loss" thoughts for you.

At some point, most of us embarking on this journey to better our health and fitness have encountered a jolt of inspiration, a fire that has been ignited underneath our butts, which propels us from the couch and into the gym / back-yard / park / whatever. With great appreciation, I look at those times, because without them, there is every possibility that nothing would have changed.

You should concentrate on your ideal weight instead of worrying overall about losing weight. Think about how much you want to weigh, why this is, and what you want to look like, for a few moments. Make the image of your ideal self as vivid as you can in your mind, and when you actually begin to believe that you are the person in your mind in the image, your subconscious can easily correct the difference by altering the simpler thing to change: the external you.

One of the aspects that you probably do not have power over is if it is a genetic factor that has caused you to put on weight and fight to lose weight again afterward. You may have always been larger than normal because you are "just that way" because of your bone structure. These genes influence the rate at which your body metabolizes food and then, of course, the fat-muscle ratio and how it is distributed in your body plays against you is affected by your appetite. You may not have power over your DNA makeup, but you do have power over how you can treat it from here. Don't get me wrong: awareness is power, and you can make better lifestyle decisions when you are armed with this ability. Don't place unreasonable pressure on yourself. It's not worth it, because if you don't meet these unattainable goals, it makes you feel worse. Accept yourself and know that you are perfect just the way you are. Yes, you will have to be cautious about what you eat and how much of it you eat and what you eat in tandem with workout routines, but remember to take a break once in a while, cheat a little here and there, and then get back to watching what you eat. You would be absolutely depressed if you do not allow yourself the occasional indulgence here and there, and, like with any strict diet, you would give up, overindulge and put on more weight again. You need to find the balance the makes you satisfied with your body and your taste buds.

For most individuals, this is the most common downfall. Many people who wanted to lose weight desperately end up opting for the easiest and least sustainable ways, such as diet pills or intense dieting. Quite often, the mentality is quickly losing weight now and thinking about what happens after giving up on the "magic bullet" later. The issue with such a mentality is that later it will just set you up for more suffering because the weight will pile back on again. Without depending on drastic steps, your attitude should embrace permanent lifestyle changes that are effective and can lead to permanent weight loss. Another mentality inside yourself is questioning; basically, you cannot even imagine yourself in a different body, soyou can't even muster the effort to make it happen. You need to understand what has to be achieved to meet your goals after setting your targets. You can't just presume that, once your priorities are set, everything is going to fall in place. To bring you closer to your target, particular tasks have to be carried out; it is as easy as that. It is best to contact a local personal trainer, who is great at supporting people in this field, if you do not have enough expertise or experience in this area.

There are so many factors that can cause weight gain; it can be a genetic factor, emotional eating, or even ignorance. As promised in the book, I mentioned and explained many factors and techniques that would help you to achieve your goals. The mindset to change your body is a great starting point for achieving your desired body. When you understand the secrets to weight loss and the techniques to achieving this through self-hypnosis, then the healthy and enviable will be achievable. You should understand that if you want to achieve something, you set the goals, change your mindset to support your aims, and work towards them; nothing can then stop you from accomplishing your goal.

Good luck as you achieve the body you want.

Printed in Great Britain
by Amazon

19487468R00078